DR. LONNIE MOORE

13 DYNAMIC LESSONS ON COPING WITH TIMES OF ISOLATION

Cavemen
AND CAVES
OF THE *Bible*

The Cavemen of The Bible is dedicated to my wife, Gail.
She has been the best Cavewoman this Caveman could
possibly have.
There has not been a cave experience in our lives that
we have not explored together.

Contents

Preface

2020 was a year described by one word, PANDEMIC. All that transpired during the year left most people desiring to put the year into the cave they were plunged into and try to forget it. We do not know what this year holds for us. Who knows, this year could be worse. It seems that we are being more and more isolated. When our country was shut down for months and our churches were told to close, many stated that it seemed we were living in caves.

It was a difficult time. It was a new experience for so many. Many did not know how to deal with living in a cave. The Lord reminded me that His people have often been forced, by circumstances beyond their control, to resort to caves. The Bible holds many exciting, adventurous, as well as troubling accounts of cavemen and their caves. God put many of His choice servants in caverned classrooms to make them *"approved unto God."* There were great men and women mentioned with their caves such as Abraham and Sarah, Isaac and Rebecca, Jacob and Leah, Gideon, Jonathan, Moses, Elijah, Lazarus, Obadiah and many more. Thus, I began a series of messages to encourage our people on "How to Behave in the Cave." This series lasted even after we were able to hold services again.

The list of caves used in this book is not exhaustive. Several others could have been used and perhaps you will be encouraged to explore others that I have not used in this study. There are 13 lessons in this book which are intended to give some encouragement to patiently endure and transform your cave into a Caverned Classroom. A good student will not only gain insight and instruction from the Master Teacher, but hopefully will help others to become adequate spelunkers. One word of caution however, is that there are no two caves alike. You must not judge another's cave experience by your own. Caves come in all sizes, depths and dangers. Some people have entered a mole tunnel and described it as Mammoth Cave!

I was encouraged by my study to discover that no cave that was mentioned in the Bible was permanent. Though you may find your cave to be necessary, don't feel that it is permanent. Though you may feel isolated, many of the Cavemen of the Bible found the presence of God and came out with the Glory of God upon them. David named one of his caves, "Under the Shadow of Thy Wings." Another warning is needed here. David also called one of his caves a "prison."

If you are in a cave, be sure it is God who put you there. Many cave dwellers of the Bible resorted to caves out of cowardice, rather than courage and fear, rather than faith. Accept God's timing and teaching. Remember, we will stand shoulder to shoulder to some of the greatest cavemen and women at the Judgment Seat of Christ. I want us to have a good day that day!

Hebrews 11:32-40
32 - And what shall I more say? for the time would fail me to tell of Gedeon, and of Barak, and of Samson, and of Jephthae; of David also, and Samuel, and of the

prophets:

33 - Who through faith subdued kingdoms, wrought righteousness, obtained promises, stopped the mouths of lions,

34 - Quenched the violence of fire, escaped the edge of the sword, out of weakness were made strong, waxed valiant in fight, turned to flight the armies of the aliens.

35 - Women received their dead raised to life again: and others were tortured, not accepting deliverance; that they might obtain a better resurrection:

36 - And others had trial of cruel mockings and scourgings, yea, moreover of bonds and imprisonment:

37 - They were stoned, they were sawn asunder, were tempted, were slain with the sword: they wandered about in sheepskins and goatskins; being destitute, afflicted, tormented;

38 - (Of whom the world was not worthy:) they wandered in deserts, and in mountains, and in dens and caves of the earth.

39 - And these all, having obtained a good report through faith, received not the promise:

40 - God having provided some better thing for us, that they without us should not be made perfect.

CHAPTER 1

The Cave of Adullam

How to Behave in the Cave

Psalm 34 and 1 Samuel 21:11-22:2

There once was a man who was betrayed by his employer, to whom he had been very loyal and faithful. Because of the deceitful dealings of his boss, he not only lost his job, but his boss tried to destroy him. The man became a fugitive, lost his home, and for refuge, was forced to live in a cave. That man was David.

Notice the title and introduction of Psalm 34 that is given: "A Psalm of David, when he changed his behavior before Abimelech; who drove him away, and he departed." David is on his way into the cave of Adullam, found in 1 Samuel 21:11-22:1-2. He is fleeing from King Saul, then from the Philistines, and has more troubles than Jimmy Carter has peanuts. Psalm 34:19 tells us, "Many are the afflictions of the righteous: but the LORD delivereth him out of them all." In our Christian life, it seems we are often in a cave. This Psalm is a cave Psalm. A cave is not a pleasant place to live. It was probably cold, dark, lonely, and spooky!

In verse 6, David found himself in the cave and spoke of himself as a "poor man." This phrase literally means a man depressed in mind and afflicted by circumstances. Is that you? Are you discouraged or afflicted by what is going on around you? This is not necessarily a bad thing. Jesus said in Matthew 5:3, "Blessed are the poor in spirit: for theirs is the kingdom of heaven." David's heart was broken, but in verse 18 we read, "The LORD is nigh unto them that are of a broken heart; and saveth such as be of a contrite spirit."

What could put us in a cave? Sometimes our finances bring us to the cave. David didn't have a roof over his head. He had lost everything financially. All his family had left their farms and pastures. Sometimes it is our foes that put us there (Psalm 120:7). David had a great enemy chasing him. Sometimes, it causes our families to be affected as well. Other times, it is fear that puts us in the cave. We must not allow fear and anxiety to make us flee, but must remember that God is still on the throne.

When we read in 1 Samuel 22:1-2, we find that David does not dwell there alone. His family and four hundred men were with him in the cave. It was probably a little crowded! That cave sounds like a Baptist church: those who were in distress, those in debt, and those who were discontented (1 Samuel 22:2).

David had to have the right attitude in the cave. Here in Psalm 34, he laid out some rules or admonitions for all those who would be in the cave. This is such an encouraging Psalm even though it was written in a cave. He was determined to make the best of his situation. How should we behave in the cave?

We must look to the Lord in our cave experiences (Psalm 34:4-5). David did so in Psalm 57:1, "Be merciful unto me, O God, be merciful unto me: for my soul trusteth in thee: yea, in the shadow of thy wings will I make my refuge, until these calamities be overpast."

Why did he go into the cave? Because of the calamities (circumstances) that drove him there. But David had determined to look at the cave as being under the shadow of the wings of the Lord.

We must probe the Word of God. In verse 4, David said, "I sought the LORD,.. ." There's nothing that will help me discover truth more than to be in need of answers. I've never had a question that the Word of God didn't answer clearly!

We must pray for His presence and direction. Notice in verse 6 he says, "This poor man cried, and the LORD heard him, and saved him out of all his troubles." We mustn't try to run out into the dark, when we don't know where we're going. We must stay right where we're at, get into the Word of God, and pray. The Lord will make it known to us through His Word. People will give us their opinion, but they will lead us astray. We must make sure to get our answer from the Lord. He'll give us the truth right out of the Word of God.

We must praise the Lord. In Psalm 34:1-3 David said, "I will bless the LORD at all times: his praise shall continually be in my mouth. My soul shall make her boast in the LORD: the humble shall hear thereof, and be glad. O magnify the LORD with me, and let us exalt his name together.". David said it didn't matter where he was at, he was going to praise the Lord! God is good! He makes no mistakes! Let's lift Him up!

We must place our faith in the promise for provision. "O taste and see that the LORD is good: blessed is the man that trusteth in him. O fear the LORD, ye his saints, for there is no want to them that fear him. The young lions do lack, and suffer hunger: but they that seek the LORD shall not want any good thing" (Psalm 34:8-10). Later on in his life, David said, "I have been young, and now am old; yet have I not seen the righteous forsaken, nor his seed begging bread" (Psalm 37:25). Then David determined to have a good day in the cave. We might as well have a good day, for a good day is better than a bad day! Why not go ahead and enjoy it? 1 Thessalonians 5:18 commands us: "In everything give thanks: for this is the will of God in Christ Jesus concerning you." How can we have a good day in our cave?

Let's be careful of what we say in the cave. Verse 13 commands us, "Keep thy tongue from evil, and thy lips from speaking guile." David told his men they weren't going to be critical, let bitterness come out of their mouths, or allow the negative to dominate their speech. We must not complain - not about our families, jobs, houses, or churches. We could lose them all. We mustn't be deceitful with others or ourselves. We say, "I don't deserve to be in a cave!" No, we don't; we deserve to be in Hell.

Let's be careful of who or what we have in the cave. Verse 14 tells us, "Depart from evil, and do good." That means be done with it! We must be on guard. David told them to get the habits and problems with their old flesh out of the cave. And if we throw it out, we must not put a rope on it so that we can pull it back into the cave later. Who are our companions with us in the cave? We must make sure to have Jesus and the right people with us. We mustn't allow the flesh, the world, and the devil to crawl into the cave.

Let's behave in the cave. He said, "Do good." The

best thing we can do in the cave is find a way to help someone else. We must get our minds off of ourselves. Encourage others!

Let's be hospitable in the cave. "Seek peace, and pursue it" (Psalm 34:14). Sometimes, peace is hard to find, but we must pursue it. Let's be those who bring peace and not division.

Finally, David determined to pave the way for others to have a good day in the cave. David found himself in the cave, but then here came his family, his friends, and those who found themselves discouraged. God allowed David to be in the cave, because He knew there would be four hundred others who would need some encouragement. How can we pave the way?

Pave the way for others to praise the Lord. When we praise the Lord, it becomes contagious, and soon others will praise Him as well. David said in verse 3, "O magnify the LORD with me, and let us exalt his name together."

Pave the way for others to trust Him. Verse 4 says, "I sought the LORD, and he heard me, and delivered me from all my fears." Verse 10 promises, "The young lions do lack, and suffer hunger: but they that seek the LORD shall not want any good thing."

Pave the way for others to fear the Lord. Fear means "to stand in awe." David, in verse 11, says, "Come, ye children, hearken unto me: I will teach you the fear of the LORD." Let's teach others to be still and stand in awe of the Lord.

Pave the way for others to live the good life. Life is really just what we make of it. If we're bitter, life is going to be bad. "What man is he that desireth life, and loveth many days, that he may see good?" (Psalm 34:12).

Pave the way for others to know the right way from the wrong way. This is a good time to teach our children. Verses 21 and 22 say, "Evil shall slay the wicked: and they that hate the righteous shall be desolate. The LORD redeemeth the soul of his servants: and none of them that trust in him shall be desolate."

Pave the way for others to allow the Lord to give them a song. Psalms 34, 57, and 142 are songs that were written in the cave. God can give us a song in the night. We can find Him to be the dearest to us in our cave experiences.

CHAPTER 2
Caveman David

The Cave of Discipleship
Psalm 57

The cave experience Psalms were written by David, regarding his Cave of Adullam experiences. Psalm 56 was written on his way to the cave, Psalm 34 upon arrival, and Psalms 57 and 142 were written within the cave.

These cave experiences were temporary. You may be facing a cave experience and may have some questions as to why you had to endure this situation at all, but God knows. Sometimes He allows these experiences to happen in order to help us. Don't allow the cave experience to be a wasted one. God may give you a song or a blessing, but surely God will bring you out with greater usefulness to Him than before you went into the cave.

For David, the cave experiences were necessary, just like they are for you and me. You may be asking, "Why am I here?" No doubt, David asked the same question. You're not there by coincidence. If you are in a cave experience by no choice of your own, then accept it as Divine Providence. Let's quit complaining and find out what God is trying to teach us. For David, it was necessary that he might "endure hardness as a good soldier." The difficult experiences in his life were what made him become the greatest king Israel had ever known. God may be preparing you through this experience for something far greater than you have ever accomplished.

Let's look at this Psalm:

"Be merciful unto me, O God, be merciful unto me: for my soul trusteth in thee: yea, in the shadow of thy wings will I make my refuge, until these calamities be overpast. I will cry unto God most high; unto God that performeth all things for me. He shall send from heaven, and save me from the reproach of him that would swallow me up. Selah. God shall send forth his mercy and his truth. My soul is among lions: and I lie even among them that are set on fire, even the sons of men, whose teeth are spears and arrows, and their tongue as a sharp sword. Be thou exalted, O God, above the heavens; let thy glory be above all the earth. They have prepared a net for my steps; my soul is bowed down: they have digged a pit before me, into the midst whereof they are fallen themselves. Selah. My heart is fixed, O God, my heart is fixed; I will sing and give praise. Awake up, my glory; awake, psaltery and harp: I myself will awake early. I will praise thee, O Lord, among the people: I will sing unto thee among the nations. For thy mercy is great unto the heavens, and thy truth unto the clouds. Be thou exalted, O God, above the heavens: let thy glory be above all the earth."

The Complexities of David's Life

Consider the complexity of David's life. His life was always changing; and, with so many changes, it is difficult to really get comfortable in life. Solomon wrote that he had everything that could be obtained in life, (entertainment, gardens, servants, palaces, wealth, storehouses full of treasures, etc.); yet, in Ecclesiastes, he exclaimed it was all vanity. He described old age, a time that should have been a time of comfort, as pathetic and depressing. Because life is always changing, we cannot become too comfortable.

David went from the solitude of being a shepherd boy to the anointing of becoming the chosen one. He went from playing his harp to pacify the sheep, to playing to pacify a demonic, deranged king. What an extreme change of scenery for David! He went from fighting bears and lions with no fanfare to fighting the giant, Goliath, between two on-looking armies of thousands. He took on Goliath, took off his head, and the cheers began to go up. Both of those armies began writing songs about David. He became the theme of the pop songs of his day, "Saul hath slain his thousands, and David his ten thousands!" No doubt, this notoriety affected David.

He went from obscurity to becoming the desire of the nation. He went from absolute dependence upon God to the natural dependence upon self, and why not? He realized he was a handsome, talented musician; a singer and songwriter; a skillful, athletic, tactful, and innocent man. He went from assuming he was just an ordinary young man who needed God, to realizing he had talents and abilities upon which he became reliant instead of upon God. He went from the place where he had friends and no foes, to a place with foes and no friends.

The Complicity of David

Consider David's complicity with the Philistines. He began to do in the flesh what he had done by the power of the Holy Spirit. God may allow us to come to the end of ourselves to realize that our flesh cannot accomplish what God intended to be accomplished by His Spirit. "...Not by might, nor by power, but by my spirit, saith the LORD of hosts" (Zechariah 4:6). God said He would use that which was nothing to confound the mighty and the foolish to confound the wise. I believe that is what God was trying to get David to understand. God had not chosen him because of all the abilities he had, for God had wrought all of his abilities in him. 1 Samuel 16:13 says, "Then Samuel took the horn of oil, and anointed him in the midst of his brethren: and the Spirit of the LORD came upon David from that day forward…" From that day forward David experienced the Holy Spirit's power; but through much success, he came to rely upon himself. Let me give you some examples:

In I Samuel 21 David, fleeing from Saul, went to the city of Nob. He told Ahimelech, the priest, he needed a weapon. No doubt the priest wondered why he needed a sword, when he was able to take down Goliath without one. David boldly said to the giant, "Thou comest to me with a sword...but I come to thee in the name of the LORD." (1 Samuel 17:45). What a great difference between the two weapons of war, man's sword, and the Sword of the Lord! Ahimelech tells David that the sword of Goliath was there. For his self-preservation, David was less than truthful with this man of God. He told Ahimelech that King Saul had sent him on some business. When circumstances in your life become difficult, do you find yourself bending the truth a little? God can still take care of us despite the circumstances. We don't have to "help God out" by bending the truth and making compromises in our testimony. David's dishonesty cost Ahimelech his life, along with the lives of all those in that city. When we bend the truth, we affect the lives of others.

Next we see David depending upon the sword that had failed Goliath. He knew he couldn't use that huge sword. He compromised with the enemy. He takes Goliath's sword to Gath, the hometown of the Philistine champion. Perhaps to impress the King of Gath, he presents the sword in exchange for a place of refuge and hiding from Saul. The Lord had been his refuge and secret place from troubles and enemies. Soon he would flee to the cave and testify, "… in the shadow of thy wings will I make my refuge, until these calamities be overpast." He did everything his own way without seeking God's will. He did it in the power and energy of the flesh, and found himself in great trouble. Perhaps he tried to trade liberty for security. Here in America, so much of what you and I put our faith and dependence on is in trouble. Our economics, healthcare system, government, elections and so much more are in serious trouble. God may be bringing us to a position where we realize we need the Great Physician! We need the One who owns the cattle on a thousand hills, The King of Kings and LORD of Lords, The Almighty Maker, to meet our needs and be our supply and govern our lives! We are losing the great liberties in our country today, because we want to feel safe and secure. We think, "Who needs God when we've got government?" Before this is over, we may emerge from the cave realizing we've got God, and He is all we need.

The Necessity of David's Cave

Consider the necessity of David's cave. Everything we've experienced, God has allowed. Job told his wife, "What? shall we receive good at the hand of God, and shall we not receive evil?" (Job 2:10). We know that all things work together for our good and His glory. That is still in the Book (Romans 8:28)! We can't be afraid of things on this earth. We must fear the Lord. God brought David to the place in his life where he could rely upon Him. So what was the necessity of this cave? God allowed David to be socially distanced from friends, family, and admirers. God brought him away from all of that. He may allow us to be separated for a while. He may get us away from all the hustle and bustle of our lives, socially distancing us from ourselves to a divine intimacy with Himself.

It would do us well, as Paul told the church of Corinth in 2 Corinthians 6:17, to "come out from among them, and be ye separate, saith the Lord, and touch not the unclean thing; and I will receive you." Sometimes, God wants us alone. David put it so beautifully in *Psalm 57:1,* "Be merciful unto me, O God, be merciful unto me: for my soul trusteth in thee: yea, in the shadow of thy wings will I make my refuge, until these calamities be overpast." That's what we all need in our cave experiences. Yes, we need social distancing. May it help us to get a divine intimacy with the Lord. James 4:8 tells us, "Draw nigh to God, and he will draw nigh to you." The devil will try everything he can to socially distance you from the Lord, but dear Christian, he can't separate you from Him. Romans 8:35 says,"Who shall separate us from the love of Christ?" He said that even death cannot separate us!

The Conformity of David

He made his cave a prayer room. What can the cave do for us? For one thing, David became more prayerful. Let us turn our caves into prayer rooms where we get a hold of God, get into His presence, come before Him with our needs, cast all our cares upon Him, and cry "Be merciful unto me, O God, be merciful unto me: for my soul trusteth in thee" (Psalm 57:1). Most of us don't pray as we should until we get in the cave.

He made his cave a safe haven. A conformity that took place in David was a spiritual awareness of his adversaries. Notice verses 3-4, "He shall send from heaven, and save me from the reproach of him that would swallow me up. Selah. God shall send forth his mercy and his truth. My soul is among lions: and I lie even among them that are set on fire, even the sons of men, whose teeth are spears and arrows, and their tongue a sharp sword." David describes "the roaring lion walking about seeking whom he may devour" (1 Peter 5:8) and the flaming fire of the fallen angels. David became incredibly aware of the one who was truly his enemy. Satan will use anyone available to do his dirty work, but David realized who was truly behind it. The necessity of the cave at times is to open up our spiritual awareness. We must understand when there is a bad spirit trying to influence us. Turn your cave into a safe haven under His wings.

He made his cave an observatory. Another conformity the cave accomplished in David's life was eternal vision. Maybe God wants to turn your cave into an observatory, where you can see beyond the end of your nose. David came to realize he was not going to stay in the cave. This was not the final chapter in his life. There was more to the book that was to be written. There was a future ahead that David was able to see. We need to lift up our eyes. There's more to be done with our lives. We are not a victim of our circumstances. We are more than conquerors! There may be a time in the cave, if you get close to God, that He will open your eyes and help you to see out the end of that tunnel.

He made his cave a musical hall. The conformity the cave brought in David's life was to give thanksgiving and praise. He transformed his cave into a musical hall. The acoustics in the cave are amplified. It is a wonderful experience! "My heart is fixed, O God, my heart is fixed; I will sing and give praise. Awake up, my glory; awake, psaltery and harp: I myself will awake early. I will praise thee, O Lord, among the people: I will sing unto thee among the nations" (Psalm 57:7-9). Stop it right now! If you have a tendency to complain about your circumstances, the best thing you can do is stop, and start praising the Lord. 1 Thessalonians 5:18 says, "In everything give thanks: for this is the will of God in Christ Jesus concerning you." Have you thanked the Lord for your cave? Have you thanked Him for the things you've had to do without lately that you had become dependent upon (toilet paper)? Thank Him for being such a good God! Start making a joyful noise unto the Lord!

He made his cave a command center. It appears the cave experience recommissioned David. He said, "I've got a future ahead!" Notice the "I wills" of David. <u>I will awake early</u>. He decided to get up and get at it! He was going to be productive. <u>I will praise thee among the people</u>. I'm going to lead the children of Israel in praise. <u>I will sing to the nations</u>. The last thing Jesus said to us was "go ye into all the world" (Matthew 28:18-20). We're not confined to the cave. We need to turn our cave into a command center to get out the Gospel.

The Futurity of David's Cave

Lastly, let's consider the future that God was preparing David for during his cave experience. There would be times in David's life when he would wish to be back in this cave. There were experiences of heartache, of losing everything he had, of his children breaking his heart and seeking his life, of facing giants, and of a divided kingdom and civil war! He needed this cave to prepare him for those times.

If you are in this Cave of Discipleship, learn what God is teaching you now. Gain the experience you need for more difficult times. Above all, discover your cave, to be as David said, "…in the shadow of thy wings will I make my refuge, until these calamities be overpast."

CHAPTER 3
The Cave of Desolation

Adullam "Justice of The People"
Psalm 142

David wrote this Psalm when he was in the cave of Adullam. We find the circumstances behind this Psalm in I Samuel 22. He had fears; he had foes who were hunting for his life; he had financial trouble; he had friends and family for whom he was concerned. Maybe, right now, you don't know what you are going to do. You feel like you have more responsibilities than you can handle. The fear of failure, perhaps, has put you in that cave situation. But if you will draw nigh to God, He will draw nigh to you. He may, as He did for David, give you a song in the night. No matter what you're going through, none of it takes God by surprise. It's all in His plan.

David wrote three Psalms while in the cave of Adullam. Psalm 34 was a psalm of instruction for the cave. Psalm 57 was a psalm of the experiences and hope found in the cave. Then Psalm 142 seems to be the psalm of desperation.

I don't know if you have reached the depths of despair, but sometimes it's the depths of despair that bring us to a complete yielding: surrender, submission, and "casting all your care upon Him" (I Peter 5:7). David by the end of this Psalm learned to cast it all on the Lord.

Listen to David's earnestness in Psalm 142:

"I cried unto the LORD with my voice; with my voice unto the LORD did I make my supplication. I poured out my complaint before him; I shewed before him my trouble. When my spirit was overwhelmed within me, then thou knewest my path. In the way wherein I walked have they privily laid a snare for me. I looked on my right hand, and beheld, but there was no man that would know me: refuge failed me; no man cared for my soul. I cried unto thee, O LORD: I said, Thou art my refuge and portion in the land of the living. Attend unto my cry; for I am brought very low: deliver me from my persecutors; for they are stronger than I. Bring my soul out of prison, that I may praise thy name: the righteous shall compass me about; for thou shalt deal bountifully with me."

Let's look at David's cry, his care, and the casting of his care. We need to come to the point that we become desperate: to the point that we realize we can do nothing about the situation without Him. I don't know how deep you are into despair, but I hope it is deep enough that you've come to the place of utter dependence upon the Lord.

David's cry was not a whimper. The word "cry" means to shriek from anguish or danger. How much do you really want revival? How much do you really want God to turn things around in your life and bring you out of the cave? When you come to the place of desperation, you'll cry out to God. I don't know about you, but I don't like to ask anyone for help. I've done without and have missed opportunities many times in my life, because I wouldn't just say, "Help me." Sometimes, help passed me by. Maybe it was because of my pride that I wouldn't say: "Would you please help me? Would you please meet the need that I have?" I didn't want people to know I was in need. Sometimes, I think it to be a weakness. But dear friend, may I say that in your time of desperation, it is no weakness to cry out to God.

Make sure the direction of your cry is right. Some people have no problem with crying, or as David put it in verse 2, complaining to anyone who will listen to them. Instead of burdening others with things they can do nothing about, why not take your cry to the Lord? Often we take our burdens to others who only add to our burden. Take it instead to the Lord, the self-existent One. He not only has everything He needs to exist, but everything you need as well.

Notice the display of David's cry. "With my voice unto the LORD did I make my supplication." (Verse 1). The word "supplication" means to bend or stoop; to seek favor. He's not complaining as we often do, "God, you know I deserve better than this!" If we got what we deserved, we'd all be in Hell. He's bowed down in worship before the Lord. If you want to make a difference with your cry, your position, your display of your cry has so much to do with it. If you're saying, "God, why won't you give me what I want?!", you're not going to get out of that situation. But if you humble yourself before Him, "a broken and a contrite heart, O God, thou wilt not despise" (Psalm 51:17). David learned the secret of it all!

Then look at the declaration of his cry in verse two: "I poured out my complaint before him; I shewed before him my trouble." That phrase "poured out" means to gush; to empty oneself. If you want to be filled with God, you're going to have to be poured out. Come to the end of yourself and be emptied before Him. But so often we're so full of ourselves that we can't receive anything that God would pour into us. We found that the declaration of his cry was to be poured out. He poured out his complaint before Him. The word complaint means anxieties. The things that troubled him the most, he poured out before the Lord. Then he "shewed before him [his] trouble." The word "shewed" means to confront openly; to expose. There were some things that God was trying to remove from David's life. There were things deep within his soul that needed to be exposed. If God brings you to that place, be willing to be exposed before Him. Come to the place where you say, "Sweet Holy Spirit, show the excess in my life. Show the ugliness, and perhaps that which I cannot see but others do see."

Do you really want your situation to change? Notice the despair of his cry in verse three: "When my spirit was overwhelmed within me, then thou knewest my path. In the way wherein I walked have they privily laid a snare for me." The word "overwhelmed" means to be enveloped in darkness. There was no light in the cave. Fainting is described by some as everything growing dark or the light going out. This was how David felt. We must get to that point of desperation before God. For when we get to the point that we can't, that's when God can! God was about to bring David up out of this cave and do great things in his life, but he had to get desperate.

We've looked at his cry; now let's look at his care. What were the cares, those anxieties that were consuming him? First of all, no man cared. "I looked on my right hand, and beheld, but there was no man that would know me: refuge failed me; no man cared for my soul" (verse 4). I believe that is the greatest desperation anyone can experience: the fear that no one cares.

Only the right hand is mentioned. The right hand is a reference to his strength. David says, "I looked to those who were strong, to those who I thought had the strength to help me." But David found that no one would pay attention or recognize him. David sought refuge in city after city, but they failed him (I Samuel 18-21). Then he summed it up with "no one cared for my soul." That is one of the saddest phrases in the Bible. It means to feel absolutely abandoned.

It has seemed to me that, during this pandemic, we have lost our voice. The media has become the voice of our enemies. Our elected officials cannot be trusted to represent us. With the many injustices and apparent gross, major fraud of our election, no one in authority seems to listen or care. Will America survive? What can we do? Are we doomed in our Cave of Desolation?

But wait! Standing somewhere in the shadows, for David, there was Jesus! For you and I, standing somewhere in the shadows, we'll find Jesus!

 Songs often minister to me in my times of need. In some of my dark hours, I have sung one of my favorite songs, <u>Standing Somewhere in the Shadows You'll Find Jesus</u>.

Many songs that minister to our hearts in times of sorrow come out of heartache and sorrow. Like David, who was given "songs in the night," this song was written in 1943 by Jack Rollings. He was a pastor and was going through a time of heartache and disappointment. God gave him a song in his dark hours. He had often preached about how the Lord could sustain and help us in times of trial. But when troubles and trials came into his life personally, his faith was shaken for a time. He began to doubt God's care. He wondered if God really cared about what was happening to him.

During his dark trial he received a letter from a fellow pastor friend named A. P. Gouthrey, who had heard of Jack's troubles and assured him of his prayers. The letter helped restore his faith in the Lord. He assured the struggling servant of God that even in the darkest times, the Lord is there. He wrote, "Standing somewhere in the shadows you'll find Jesus." That statement spoke to the heart of Pastor Rollings. Even in the dark time he'd been going through, the Lord was with him, and could minister graciously to him.

Verse 1
Are your crosses too heavy to carry;
And burdens too heavy to bear?
Are there heartaches and tears and anguish;
And there's no one who seems to care?

Verse 2
Are there shadows of deep disappointment,

And trusts that have proven untrue?
Has the darkness of night settled round you
Has your hope and your faith wavered too?

Verse 3
Has the storm over shadowed your sunshine,
And life lost attraction for you?
Have the dreams that you cherished been broken,
Is your soul filled with bitterness too?

Chorus
Standing somewhere in the shadows you'll find Jesus,
He's the Friend who always cares and understands.
Standing somewhere in the shadows you will find Him
And you'll know Him by the nail prints in His hands.

In verse five, David says, "I cried unto thee, O LORD: I said, Thou art my refuge and my portion in the land of the living." When he sought man for refuge it failed, but when he sought God he found a shelter in the time of storm. That word "portion" means allotment of possession. God has given you a life. Do you realize that everything you have, God has given you as a possession? No one else can provide your purpose of life. You have been allotted a number of days. You have been allotted your resources. You have been allotted all of your circumstances. God is in control of it all!

It's very frustrating to think you are the purpose and the allotment. But when you come to complete reliance upon Him for every day, you'll quit fearing. "For God hath not given us the spirit of fear; but of power, and of love, and of a sound mind" (II Timothy 1:7).

We've seen David's cry and his care; lastly, let's look at the casting of his cares. David had some adversaries. Verse 6 says, "Attend unto my cry; for I am brought very low: deliver me from my persecutors; for they are stronger than I." Yes, we have an adversary as well: that old Devil (I Peter 5:8). But the answer comes from I Peter 5:7, "Casting all your care upon him; for he careth for you."

Look at David's position in the casting of his care. He said, "I am brought very low." To realize you are not the chief any more, and you are unworthy, unfit, that's alright. His persecutors were stronger than he was. But when you come to realize all your adversaries are stronger than you, you might come to the place where you realize you have a Friend. You have One that is stronger than all your adversaries and stronger than you.

Notice his prison. "Bring my soul out of prison..." he says in verse seven. Do you feel as if your circumstances have gotten you to the place where you have no liberty or freedom? The word prison means a dungeon. I believe he is using it to describe the cave he is in. He is saying, "Lord, bring me out of this dungeon. This cave that I'm in is lacking freedom. I'm restricted here. I can't do as I please any more. Bring me out of this prison!"

Then notice his praise. He said in verse 7, "that I may praise thy name." Why do you want out of your cave? Is it so you can go back to your pleasures? If so, you may never get out of that cave. But you must get to the point that you're willing to say, "Lord, deliver me from this cave, so that I may praise Your name and give you all the glory!"

Lastly, notice his promise. He doesn't end this Psalm in despair. He said, "the righteous shall compass me about; for thou shalt deal bountifully with me." We see two things he is promised. First, the congregation. Do you long to be back among the brothers and sisters in Christ? God sometimes causes us to be desolate and alone that we might desire to be back among His people. Maybe we haven't appreciated our churches as much as we should. Be careful not to be critical of anything you have because you could lose it, especially the church. Second, he is promised God's blessing. Good days are ahead of us despite our circumstances.

This was the cave of desperation, but it all became the cave of God's blessing. As Winston Churchill said in the deepest, darkest hour of World War II, when England was being bombed night after night, "This is England's finest hour." Church, this may be our finest hour. Let's look to Him and let God be God.

CHAPTER 4

Caveman David

The Cave of Deliverance and Revival

"A Drink of Water from the Well of Bethlehem"

II Samuel 23

The Cave of Adullam, for David, was a classroom. There he received, from THE MASTER TEACHER, leadership training that transformed the former shepherd boy (and now warrior) into the greatest king Israel would ever know. In this caverned classroom, David developed an intimate master/pupil relationship. David asked very intense questions and expressed his deepest heart-felt emotions, fears, and anxieties. He expected answers, as well as actions, from Almighty God.

David had often retreated to the Cave of Adullam, not for learning, but for refuge. However, in every retreat, David found more than refuge; he found God. He came out of the Cave of Learning assured of the will of God for his life. In the account found in 1 Chronicles 11:15, this place was called "The Rock." Later on, David referred to Jesus as "The Rock." "And he said, **The LORD is my rock**, and my fortress, and my deliverer" (2 Samuel 22:2).

In Psalm 57:1, David referred to this Cave of Adullam as being in "The Shadow of Thy Wings." David said, "Be merciful unto me, O God, be merciful unto me:

for my soul trusteth in thee: yea, in **the shadow of thy wings** will I make my refuge, until these calamities be overpast."

This cave was "the rock" which signified that God is our protection, but He is also our refuge, "the shadow of thy wings," in which we can hide.

However, in times of discouragement and depression, David referred to the Cave of Adullam as being a "prison." Psalm 142:7 says, "Bring my soul out of **prison**, that I may praise thy name: the righteous shall compass me about; for thou shalt deal bountifully with me."

The inspired events of the Cave of Adullam happened between years 45 and 50 of David's life. This would be the last recorded experience for David in the Cave of Learning. This would be his final exam before graduation. He would graduate Summa Cum Laude: "with highest honors."

Amazingly, this mid-life cave experience is coupled with the last words of David. As he traces back his steps of life, he recalls this Cave of Adullam experience and the men who graduated with him. Three of them graduated Magna Cum Laude: "with high honors." This is their story as recalled by David.

David, as a boy, was anointed to be the next king of Israel. Yet, it would be over thirty years of conflicts of roller-coaster proportion and civil war, before David would be anointed king of a united Israel. David assumed his reign of peace and prosperity would now begin. But as is often the case, prosperity is followed by a Cave of Adullam experience.

In 1 Samuel 17, we find that David killed Goliath and became the song of the maidens. Then Saul became outraged, and David found himself on the run. That's when he found this cave, where he would often flee to get away from Saul or from the Philistines. But this time of fleeing, we find that he had just been anointed.

After much feasting and celebration, all of Israel dispersed to their homes. The Philistines, upon hearing of David's much celebrated coronation, invaded the land with a mighty host to seek and destroy the new king. Bethlehem, the boyhood home of David, became their headquarters with a garrison of soldiers. In defiance and mockery of David, the Philistines ate bread from "The House of Bread," (Bethlehem) and enjoyed cool refreshing water from the well of Bethlehem.

As long as Hebron and the Northern Kingdom of Israel were divided, the Philistines showed little opposition to David. However, once the kingdoms were united, the Philistines sought to destroy him.

Satan will not tolerate unity among believers. He is the master of defiance and seeks to possess every sacred place of our lives. He will drink the water of our sacred wells and scoff while he drinks. He dares you and me, to summon our God to challenge him.

Once again, David crawled into his isolated cave. Seemingly, David had failed at every turn in life. Discouraged and thirsty, David recalled the well of his boyhood home in Bethlehem. In despair, he cried out, perhaps subconsciously to God, "Oh that one would give me drink of the water of the well of Bethlehem, which is by the gate!" (2 Samuel 23:15).

There are three experiences in this cave of learning that transformed David and his infant kingdom into the greatest king and kingdom under God's heaven. Let's notice:

1. The Remembrance of David in the Cave
2. The Request of David in the Cave
3. The Revival of David from the Cave

The Remembrance of David

● **David remembers the Well**

In this statement, he is recalling a remembrance of his boyhood. Those days were carefree times.

When I was a boy, everyone had a well in their backyard. I loved drawing water from the well. There's no better water than water from a well. But I have to think all the way back to my boyhood time to remember that experience. That time in my life was good. I didn't have a care in the world. There are times now that I think, "Oh, I would love to go back to that time and drink from that well!" No doubt, this is what David was experiencing.

I would like to make an application here. For you and me, Jesus is the well by the gate! "Jesus answered and said unto her, Whosoever drinketh of this water shall thirst again: But whosoever drinketh of the water that I shall give him shall never thirst; but the water that I shall give him shall be in him a well of water springing up into everlasting life" (John 4:13).

In the culture of that day, there would be one well and it would be strategically dug to be accessible to all of the village or city. Like the well by the gate, Jesus is accessible to whosoever will come and drink, and it is free. The only expense of the water was to the one who dug the well. To all who follow for generations to come, the water is free. Jesus paid the price for you and me to drink freely. This Water of Life is free to all for every generation.

Not only was the well easily accessible, but the well was available anytime night or day. The only requirement is to come. "And the Spirit and the bride say, Come. And let him that heareth say, Come. And let him that is athirst come. And whosoever will, let him take the water of life freely" (Rev. 22:17).

Best of all, this well satisfies the thirstiest, parched soul. David knew by his own experience the well by the gate would satisfy any thirsty soul.

This well was in Bethlehem which means, "The House of Bread." Not only is Jesus "The Well" that satisfies thirst, He is "The House of Bread" that fills the starving, hungry soul. Jesus is more than a bite or even a loaf of bread, He is the whole Bakery! "And Jesus said unto them, I am the bread of life: he that cometh to me shall never hunger; and he that believeth on me shall never thirst" (John 6:35).

The well had refreshed David as a boy. Can you imagine David as a boy in his home, the house of bread, as he smells fresh bread coming out of the oven? He hears momma say, "Supper is ready! David, go to the well and draw a cool bucket of water, and let's sit down and enjoy our family supper!"

The Well refreshed David in the Cave of Adullam, as a reminder, a sign from God. Can you imagine, David now in the cave, despondent and uncertain of the future? His mind wanders to the old home place and better times. In the House of Bread, he smells fresh bread coming out of the oven. He hears momma say, "Supper is ready. David go to the well and draw a cool bucket of water, and let's sit down and enjoy our family supper!"

The Well would yet refresh him. He could not go back to those days as a boy. He must get up! He must get out of the cave! He must go to the well. He must face his enemies! With God's assurance and courage, he would once again sit down at the table, his enemies defeated, and drink and eat freely himself.

- **David remembers "The Three" that were instrumental in his conquest.**

Upon David's death bed, he recalls the three young men who encouraged him in his darkest hour in the Cave of Adullam. They gave him a drink from his old well at his home in Bethlehem. Many, with great courage and sacrifice, have motivated others to act the same. God led our church, Tabernacle Baptist Church, to challenge our governor to open our church services during the COVID-19 crisis. In Federal Court we won an unprecedented decision in just three days. We were able to open our church doors for Mother's Day! Because of our small victory, hundreds of churches were encouraged to open their doors once again and invite whosoever will, to drink from The Eternal Well that never runs dry! The three heroes whose exploits are recalled by David, encouraged him and his men to get out of the cave and conquer the land that God had promised them.

Like Mary in her lavish anointing of her Lord (John 12:3), her love and sacrificial deed has prompted untold numbers to "Pour it all on Jesus" though some may consider it a waste.

The great, personal sacrifices of Apostle Paul have encouraged untold thousands to join the victorious ranks of the redeemed. One day, they will hear from their Commander-in-Chief, "Well Done!"

So who were these mighty men of David? They are recalled by David as Adino the Eznite, Eleazar the son of Dodo the Ahohite, and Shammah the son of Agee the Hararite.

Most of the men of Israel were "gone away" (2 Samuel 23:9), but these three decided that something had to be done.

Adino annihilated 800 of the Philistines, I believe, while the other two were drawing water. Adino "smote the Philistines until his hand was weary, and his hand clave unto the sword" (2 Samuel 23:10).

Eleazar, "smote the Philistines until his hand was weary, and his hand clave unto the sword." Eleazar was the son of Dodo. If God can use the son of a Dodo, He can use anybody! "And after him was Eleazar the son of Dodo the Ahohite, one of the three mighty men with David, when they defied the Philistines that were there gathered together to battle, and the men of Israel were gone away: He arose, and smote the Philistines until his hand was weary, and his hand clave unto the sword: and the LORD wrought a great victory that day; and the people returned after him only to spoil" (2 Samuel 23:9).

Shammah, "stood in the midst of the ground and defended it, and slew the Philistines" (2 Samuel 23:12). God can use anyone who will yield themself to Him. The Apostle Paul had that mindset when he said, "But none of these things move me, neither count I my life dear unto myself, so that I might finish my course with joy, and the ministry, which I have received of the Lord Jesus, to testify the gospel of the grace of God" (Acts 20:24).

Notice the characteristics of "The Three" that God chose to spark this great conquest.

These men were loyal to God's man. In a church, God will not use self-seeking, obstinate men, but those in a church that are loyal to God's man. These men were humble men, not prideful, glory-seeking, vain men. They did not name themselves, but others called them: "The Three."

They were unselfish, self-sacrificing men, seeking the good of others. They were courageous men. They knew accomplishing their feat might cost them blood! Yet, once out of the cave, they never faltered until the drink of the well was delivered.

Perhaps the greatest characteristic of these men was their faith. Faith in a God that could take three nameless men and give them names more noble than all the mighty men of David. Faith in a God that could take a drink from the well and inspire an entire nation to take back the whole well. These men of faith trusted their fate to the hands of an Almighty God, that living or dying, God would use them. Like Jonathan, who ventured out of the caves where Israel was hiding. He offered himself by faith to God to gain a great victory. "And Jonathan said to the young man that bare his armour, Come, and let us go over unto the garrison of these uncircumcised: it may be that the LORD will work for us: for there is no restraint to the LORD to save by many or by few" (1 Samuel 14:6).

- **David remembered his enemy the Philistines, who were a type of our enemy and adversary, Satan.**

David remembered the near fatality of his beloved nation by a ruthless enemy. It was an enemy that took his beloved home and sacred well, scoffing as he took refuge in the cave. He never forgot how quickly God's people could be driven into caves with so little hope. He never forgot that faith in an omnipotent God would make him and his people overcomers.

The Request of David

- **David's request is small. His only request is for a drink.**

Oftentimes our faith is small and therefore our prayer may be small. But we must pray by faith allowing God to grow our faith and enable us to ask for "great and mighty things which thou knowest not."

Amazingly, God acted upon this desperate cry of David and answered this pitiful plea with a token or pledge to not only give him a drink from the well, but to give him the well and the whole of Bethlehem as well! Three of David's most loyal men heard the exasperated plea. God put in their heart a desire to start an avalanche of conquest, that would give to David the entire Promised Land never before possessed by Israel. The self-sacrificing act of these three men gave David courage. It was a sign to David, like was given to Gideon, of a tremendous conquest to come. This would be the last time that they would need to be in this cave. The Three, as they became known, ventured out risking their lives and made a great difference. They took on a garrison, which encouraged David and his men to take on the troop. They continued until absolute conquest. They got God's attention by choosing to do something beyond expectation.

This seemingly impossible task that these three men carried out became a sign to David. His heart was encouraged and strengthened by their faith. It doesn't matter how great or how small of a request we may ask of God; He will answer. Maybe you don't have much faith, but you can ask God for a drink from the well. If you will trust God enough to ask Him for a little bit, He'll give you the courage to ask Him for a whole lot.

Just as David desired a drink from the well of Bethlehem, we should desire a drink from Jesus. In John 4:13-14, Jesus told the woman at the well, "Whosoever drinketh of this water shall thirst again: But whosoever drinketh of the water that I shall give him shall never thirst; but the water that I shall give him shall be in him a well of water springing up into everlasting life." He is our well, but He is also our "House of Bread." John 6:35 says, "And Jesus said unto them, I am the bread of life: he that cometh to me shall never hunger; and he that believeth on me shall never thirst." No doubt David thought back to those times as a boy or as a young man when he would go home to the "House of Bread" and enjoy fresh bread from the oven. Now, he saw the Philistines in his hometown enjoying what he once did. The well refreshed David as a reminder that God was still on the throne.

- **David's faith grows and his next request is larger. David continues to make requests for conquest, each larger in faith and conquest, until God gave him the whole promised land of Israel.**

David had learned that prayer and faith were essential to advance the will of God. He prayed and he conquered "from faith to faith." He learned that "Faith is the Victory!"

"And David enquired of the LORD, saying, Shall I go up to the Philistines? wilt thou deliver them into mine hand? And the LORD said unto David, Go up: for I will doubtless deliver the Philistines into thine hand" (2 Samuel 5:19).

"And the Philistines came up yet again, and spread themselves in the valley of Rephaim. And when David enquired of the LORD, he said, Thou shalt not go up;

but fetch a compass behind them, and come upon them over against the mulberry trees. And let it be, when thou hearest the sound of a going in the tops of the mulberry trees, that then thou shalt bestir thyself: for then shall the LORD go out before thee, to smite the host of the Philistines. And David did so, as the LORD had commanded him; and smote the Philistines from Geba until thou come to Gazer" (2 Samuel 5:22-25).

The Revival of David

How did this conquest come to pass? First, David had to pray. His plea was desperate. The three were close enough in fellowship with him to hear his prayer, and then they ventured out of the cave without being ordered to go. If you're waiting on God or someone in authority to tell you what to do for God, you'll never be able to be used greatly for Him. These men chose to face, fight, and persevere against the enemy, rather than choosing to quit when met with difficulty or wounds. They chose a selfless act for others, rather than drinking the water themselves. If what you're doing is for yourself, it won't take much to discourage you; but if you have a heart for God and others, you will continue on as they did. When they brought it back to David, he determined not to drink until all could drink from the well; therefore, he poured it out before the Lord as a dedication to continue the conquest until all could freely drink.

As soon as they returned, they didn't rest on the laurels of what they had just accomplished, but got right back in the fight and led the rest of the men of Israel to finish defeating the Philistines. And they were rewarded with a "Well done!"

It was this small victory of these three men that sparked a revival that revived a discouraged, newly-crowned king. It continued until all of the Promised Land was possessed, and all of the enemies of Israel were defeated.

We need those who may be insignificant, to venture out of their caves trusting God to use them to encourage the men of God and do exploits for God. Our country needs revival! Let's take the challenge of Jonathan. "And Jonathan said to the young man that bare his armour, Come, and let us go over unto the garrison of these uncircumcised: it may be that the LORD will work for us: for there is no restraint to the LORD to save by many or by few" (1 Samuel 14:6).

We cannot go back to those days again. We must not rely upon the memory of better times. God is still on the throne. The well is still by the gate of the House of Bread. Take hold of the plow! Don't look back! Get up! Trust God! Move forward! Onward! Forward! Rally around the banner! On to the conquest! There is no reverse in this train! If we'll allow the Lord to do something in the circumstances we're in, He will give us a great conquest.

CHAPTER 5

Caveman Joseph & Jesus

The Cave of Death and the Cave that Saves!

Matthew 27:50-66

I have been in several natural caves, as well as a few man-made caves in my life. But today, we will consider the most amazing, man-made cave in which I have ever been. I wept as I stood inside an empty, hewn tomb called The Garden Tomb, believed to be the tomb of Joseph of Arimathea. We have considered several caves and cavemen and how God worked in their circumstances; however, no cave made by God or man has as much significance as the empty tomb of Joseph, or should I say, the one borrowed for three days by Jesus.

Here in this scene, we are at this man-made cave, hewn out by Joseph for himself. This cave is symbolic of each of us as sinners. We have dug our own grave ("For all have sinned, and come short of the glory of God;" Romans 3:23). Joseph deserved to be the one laid in this cave, for he was the one who had made it. We are all deserving of the grave and death (Romans 6:23, "For the wages of sin is death..."). Not only was this cave hewn by Joseph and deserved by him, but it was also reserved for him (Job 21:28-32 "...and where are the dwelling places of the wicked?...That the wicked is reserved to the day of destruction? they shall be brought forth to the day of wrath. Who shall declare his way to his face? and who shall repay him what he hath done? Yet shall he be brought to the grave, and shall remain in the tomb.") In our sin without Jesus, death and Hell are reserved for us. Then, it was preserved by him. Hebrews 9:27-28 tells us, "And as it is appointed unto men once to die, but after this the judgment: So Christ was once offered to bear the sins of many; and unto them that look for him shall he appear the second time without sin unto salvation."

This cave was made by man, but it was laid in by God. God Himself lay in that cave! In Matthew 27:54, the centurion who witnessed Jesus' death proclaimed, "Truly this was the Son of God." Philippians 2:5-11 says, "Let this mind be in you, which was also in Christ Jesus: Who, being in the form of God, thought it not robbery to be equal with God: But made himself of no reputation, and took upon him the form of a servant, and was made in the likeness of men: And being found in fashion as a man, he humbled himself, and became obedient unto death, even the death of the cross. Wherefore God also hath highly exalted him, and given him a name which is above every name: That at the name of Jesus every knee should bow, of things in heaven, and things in earth, and things under the earth; And that every tongue should confess that Jesus Christ is Lord, to the glory of God the Father. "

Before Joseph could be laid there, God was laid there. God humbled Himself and became a man. It was human hands that nailed Him to the cross. It was human hands who took Him down off the cross. It was the same God who made mountains and spilled out the sea whose hands were folded by man. Human hands wound Him in those grave linens. Human hands laid Him in this tomb. God being handled by man is amazing to me!

John the beloved, testifying of who Jesus was, said "That which was from the beginning, which we have heard, which we have seen with our eyes, which we have looked upon, and our hands have handled, of the Word of life" (1 John 1:1).

This cave saved fallen man. Jesus died for us. Romans 5:8 tells us, "But God commendeth his love toward us, in that, while we were yet sinners, Christ died for us."

Isaiah 53:3-12 "He is despised and rejected of men; a man of sorrows, and acquainted with grief: and we hid as it were our faces from him; he was despised, and we esteemed him not. Surely he hath borne our griefs, and carried our sorrows: yet we did esteem him stricken, smitten of God, and afflicted. But he was wounded for our transgressions, he was bruised for our iniquities: the chastisement of our peace was upon him; and with his stripes we are healed. All we like sheep have gone astray; we have turned every one to his own way; and the LORD hath laid on him the iniquity of us all. He was oppressed, and he was afflicted, yet he opened not his mouth: he is brought as a lamb to the slaughter, and as a sheep before her shearers is dumb, so he openeth not his mouth. He was taken from prison and from judgment: and who shall declare his generation? for he was cut off out of the land of the living: for the transgression of my people was he stricken. And he made his grave with the wicked, and with the rich in his death; because he had done no violence, neither was any deceit in his mouth. Yet it pleased the LORD to bruise him; he hath put him to grief: when thou shalt make his soul an offering for sin, he shall see his seed, he shall prolong his days, and the pleasure of the LORD shall prosper in his hand. He shall see of the travail of his soul, and shall be satisfied:

by his knowledge shall my righteous servant justify many; for he shall bear their iniquities. Therefore will I divide him a portion with the great, and he shall divide the spoil with the strong; because he hath poured out his soul unto death: and he was numbered with the transgressors; and he bare the sin of many, and made intercession for the transgressors."

He was laid in the tomb, so that you and I would never have to be laid in Hell. We have the blessed promise that we do not even have to see death (John 8:51). As Lazarus was taken and laid in Abraham's bosom (Luke 16), so we will not be laid in the grave, but in Heaven. Our bodies which once housed us may be laid somewhere, but the Bible tells us that we will "be absent from the body, and to be present with the Lord" (2 Corinthians 5:8). Jesus said in John 11:25-26, "I am the resurrection, and the life: he that believeth in me, though he were dead, yet shall he live: And whosoever liveth and believeth in me shall never die. Believest thou this?"

Because He was laid in the tomb, we are promised that we will never see corruption. Psalm 16:8-11 tells us, "I have set the LORD always before me: because he is at my right hand, I shall not be moved. Therefore my heart is glad, and my glory rejoiceth: my flesh also shall rest in hope. For thou wilt not leave my soul in hell; neither wilt thou suffer thine Holy One to see corruption. Thou wilt shew me the path of life: in thy presence is fulness of joy; at thy right hand there are pleasures for evermore." The Apostle Paul told us in Colossians 3:1, "If ye then be risen with Christ, seek those things which are above, where Christ sitteth on the right hand of God." We are risen with Him. As Christians, we do not have to fear anything, even death.

CHAPTER 6
Caveman Lazarus

**"It was death that put him in the cave...
but it was life that brought him out!"
John 11**

There were two or three caves mentioned in the Bible that were used as graves. The cave mentioned in John 11:38 is the grave of Lazarus. This chapter is one of the most heart-wrenching chapters in the Bible. It reveals the questioning of the love and devotion of Jesus to His dearest friends. Jesus states that He was glad He was not there to prevent their heartaches. This is one of the unanswered sayings of Christ. At first, it stings us to think that the Lord Jesus was glad He was not present when this family went through such pain and heartache. We have all said or felt that we were glad we were not at some event or disaster. There are people who missed a flight that crashed or a trip that went wrong. Here we hear from the lips of the One who cares more than anyone does, that He was glad not to be at a place where those He loved suffered such pain and heartache. No doubt it was extremely difficult for Mary and Martha to understand their dear Savior's delay in preventing the death of their brother and their ensuing heartache and grief.

God blessed my wife and me with four wonderful daughters who now are all grown with children of their own. When they were young, I had to physically hold and restrain each of them for a doctor to do a medical procedure on them. My daughter Leah at two years of age was severely burned and was treated for weeks by a burn specialist. I had the unpleasant task of holding her while the doctors did excruciatingly painful treatments on her. I restrained Sarah at three years of age for the doctors to stitch her head. At the age of 14, Sarah had a ruptured appendix and was hospitalized for 11 days. She begged me to not allow them to pull the drain tube from her incision. Hannah at 10, had pancreatitis and gallbladder surgery and was hospitalized for two weeks with complications. Once again, I could not intervene in the painful removal of the drain tube.

The most difficult experience for me as a father was Rebecca, my oldest, when she was 3 years of age. She was two weeks in the hospital with complications of her appendectomy. Her incision became abscessed, and the doctor had to reopen her incision to allow it to drain and stuff gauze inside the wound. Rather than put her to sleep, he asked me and two nurses to hold her down while he did the surgical procedure. I held her shoulders with my face near hers trying to comfort her. The procedure took 3 to four minutes which seemed like forever! She screamed in pain. She pleaded, looking in my eyes, over and over, "Daddy make them stop!" Each time I held my daughters was a nightmare for me. Each of them pleading for me to intercede and prevent the tormenting pain the doctor was inflicting. At the time, they did not understand. They knew I could prevent the hurt, yet would not. I wept with them, but I had to allow their inflicted pain for the doctor to make them well. I gladly would have taken their place, but I could not.

To give you the setting of this cave story, the Lord Jesus is a couple days journey from Bethany. In Bethany, Jesus had some very dear friends with whom He often would abide. It was the home of Martha, Mary, and their brother Lazarus. There the Lord Jesus would eat Martha's good cooking, and Mary would sit and listen as Jesus taught and gave His Word. Oh, how He loved them! He loved Lazarus as well, but Lazarus became ill. It was very apparent that he was going to die. There was nothing the doctors or anyone else could do, but they knew the One who could make a difference in Lazarus: Jesus. So they sent some of their friends to get word to Him. They said, in verse 3, "Lord, behold, he whom thou lovest is sick."

But Jesus made some statements that certainly they could not understand. In verse 4, He said, "This sickness is not unto death, but for the glory of God, that the Son of God might be glorified thereby." Verse 5 clearly tells us, "Now Jesus loved Martha, and her sister, and Lazarus." But He tarried; He delayed. Verse 6 says, "he abode two days still in the same place where he was." Jesus did not get in a hurry or become anxious. Though the news was very anxious and the prayers were very direct ("You've got to do something, Lord!"), still he delayed.

After He had waited, He said, "Let's go." The disciples tried to then say, "Lord, You've waited this long. There's no need to get in a hurry. You know they're going to kill us. If we go, they will seek our lives." But Jesus said, "I've got to go. I've got to awaken Lazarus out of sleep." The disciples did not understand. They thought, "If he is sleeping, he is doing well. Let him rest." Verse

14 says, "Then said Jesus unto them plainly, Lazarus is dead."

Now the question is: Why didn't Jesus do something about it? Why didn't He stop it from happening? Notice what He said to His disciples in verse 15, "And I am glad for your sakes that I was not there, to the intent ye may believe; nevertheless let us go unto him." Jesus said that He was glad He had not been there. Have you ever wondered the same about God? Perhaps you have found yourself asking, "God, where are You? Why aren't You doing something about this situation?"

You can be assured that the reason Jesus was not there was not because He did not know the seriousness of the situation. Some people think, "Well, if God really knew what was going on, He would do something." He knew the seriousness of the situation. He said, "Lazarus is sick unto death." Then He said, "Lazarus is dead." He was not ignorant. Nor was the reason He was not there, because He was too far to get there in time. "Now Bethany was nigh unto Jerusalem, about fifteen furlongs off" (verse 18). That was not far. Your cave or the problem you find yourself in, is not too far for God. If God is not acting on your timetable or according to your schedule, it is not because He's too far away to get to you.

Nor was the reason, because the family did not want Him to come. I have been asked before not to attend a funeral. But Lazarus' family wanted the Lord there. They sent to Him saying, "...he whom thou lovest is sick" (verse 3).

It was not because He did not love them. I don't know what Satan may be trying to get you to believe, but God loves you! Jesus came to the cave. Verse 38 tells us: "Jesus therefore again groaning in himself cometh to the grave. It was a cave, and a stone lay upon it." When He got there, He heard Mary and Martha saying, "Lord, if thou hadst been here, my brother had not died" (verse 21). Mary was weeping. "When Jesus therefore saw her weeping, and the Jews also weeping which came with her, he groaned in the spirit, and was troubled, And said, Where have ye laid him? They said unto him, Lord, come and see. Jesus wept. Then said the Jews, Behold how he loved him!" Jesus loved them! Not just Lazarus, but the others also. I'm glad that the Lord Jesus, as Isaiah 53:3-4 says, "was a man of sorrows, and acquainted with grief...Surely he hath borne our griefs, and carried our sorrows." Yes, "we have not an high priest which cannot be touched with the feeling of our infirmities; but was in all points tempted like as we are, yet without sin. Let us therefore come boldly unto the throne of grace, that we may obtain mercy, and find grace to help in time of need" (Hebrews 4:15-16).

Often we see that God's timing is not our timing, and His ways are not our ways. "And I am glad for your sakes that I was not there..." (verse 15). Isaiah 55:8-9 says, "For my thoughts are not your thoughts, neither are your ways my ways, saith the LORD. For as the heavens are higher than the earth, so are my ways higher than your ways, and my thoughts than your thoughts." Are there some circumstances you're questioning?

It was death that put him in the cave.

Consider that it was death that put him in the cave. This cave was a grave. Romans 6:23 says, "For the wages of sin is death." The consequence for sin is death. We have all sinned (Romans 3:23; 5:12). Because we have all sinned, we all have an appointment with death.

It was delay that brought doubt to the minds of the disciples.

It was delay that brought doubt to the minds of the disciples. It was not the grave that was delayed. You cannot delay the grave, "And as it is appointed unto men once to die, but after this the judgment;" (Hebrews 9:27). Lazarus was there at the appointed time in his life. Yes, it was sin that put him there, for it is sin that separates us from God. We cannot prevent the death of our loved ones. We must be prepared for that day. If we are ready for that day, the fear and dread will be taken away.

At the cave, there was dread. Everyone feared this cave. Fear is the enemy of faith. Fear leads to doubt; it is contagious. Martha got up in the face of Jesus and said, "Lord, if thou hadst been here, my brother had not died" (verse 21). Then Mary came and fell down at His feet and said the same thing (verse 32). There is nothing wrong with asking God "Why?", but understand the importance of how you ask, the way you ask, and the position in which you ask. Don't allow the devil to put anger and bitterness in your heart. Coming before the Lord humbly and falling at His feet will bring more answers.

It was death that put Lazarus in the cave, but it was life that brought him out!

It was death that put Lazarus in the cave, but it was life that brought him out! Verses 25 and 26 say, "Jesus said unto her, I am the resurrection, and the life: he that believeth in me, though he were dead, yet shall he live: And whosoever liveth and believeth in me shall never die. Believest thou this?" This loving Jesus, weeping as he came to the grave where the stone lay, said in verse 39, "Take ye away the stone." Martha said, "But, Lord, we can't do that!" (verse 39) There is always a "Martha" in the crowd to tell you why you can't do what God said to do. "Jesus saith unto her, Said I not unto thee, that, if thou wouldest believe, thou shouldest see the glory of God? Then they took away the stone from the place where the dead was laid. And Jesus lifted up his eyes, and said, Father, I thank thee that thou hast heard me. And I knew that thou hearest me always: but because of the people which stand by I said it, that they may believe that thou hast sent me" (verses 40-42). The Father had already heard Him, for Jesus had already known what He was going to do and had asked the Father. Jesus prayed not just for Lazarus, but for everyone who was there. Jesus is not just interested in you, but in your family. He is interested in your acquaintances. If we will let faith conquer our fear, LIFE will bring us out of the cave. "The just shall live by faith" (Romans 1:17). Have you lived long enough with your fears? It's time to live by faith!

CHAPTER 7

Caveman Elijah

The Cave of Depression

When the Up and At It, Get the Down and Outs!
I Kings 19

Elijah was a man for his times. We need men today for the times in which we live. Good men and even great men have been plagued with bouts of depression. Charles Spurgeon, Martin Luther, John Calvin, John Wesley, George Frideric Handel (composed Messiah), Abraham Lincoln, Winston Churchill, and Isaac Newton (the most famous mathematician of the 17th Century) all suffered from several "nervous breakdowns." The composer, Ludwig Van Beethoven, had bipolar disorder and wrote his most famous works during times of torment, loneliness, and suffering with psychotic delusions. He medicated himself with the only drugs available on that day to bring some relief, opium and alcohol, and died of liver disease. Terry Bradshaw, the winner of four super bowls and a successful sportscaster, writer, singer, and actor, was diagnosed with depression seven years ago and has used a combination of positive thinking, therapy, and medications to overcome the illness.

There have been great men of the Bible who had near death experiences with depression. Men of the Bible like Job, John the Baptist ("Art thou the Christ?"), and

King David who wrote in Psalm 6:2-7, "Have mercy upon me, O LORD; for I am weak: O LORD, heal me; for my bones are vexed. My soul is also sore vexed: but thou, O LORD, how long? Return, O LORD, deliver my soul: oh save me for thy mercies' sake. For in death there is no remembrance of thee: in the grave who shall give thee thanks? I am weary with my groaning; all the night make I my bed to swim; I water my couch with my tears. Mine eye is consumed because of grief; it waxeth old because of all mine enemies." Also, Abraham and Sarah, Hannah, and Jeremiah had bouts with depression. Some men I have known, good men of God, lost their battle with depression and ended their life.

The man we are going to consider in this chapter nearly lost the battle with depression. He entered into a cave to die; however, he met God in the cave. He was revived and came out of the cave energized with the power of God. Elijah was a man, like any one of us, who suffered from depression. James 5:17 says, "Elias was a man subject to like passions as we are." Passions means suffering the like with another, of like feelings or affections.

Depression is a spiritual attack from Satan. Abraham Lincoln once wrote in a letter to a friend, "A tendency to melancholy…let it be observed, is a misfortune not a fault." We often do not realize the source of depression comes from without, and not from within. Satan assaults with depression and then makes us feel guilty, which adds to the affliction.

God allows these deep descents into caves of depression and despair to bring us close to Himself. We have a

Friend in Jesus who was a man "despised and rejected of men; a man of sorrows, and acquainted with grief" (Isaiah 53:3). Depression should cause us to administer the mind healing potion of I Peter 5:7, "Casting all your care upon him; for he careth for you." We need to draw nigh to the One who promised, "…we have not an high priest which cannot be touched with the feeling of our infirmities; but was in all points tempted like as we are, yet without sin" (Hebrews 4:15).

Elijah had a busy, eventful life. He seemed to be the center of every major event, whether catastrophe or controversy. He seemed to be always on the go, always up and at it. Suddenly, it all changed. Instead of running *for* God, he seemed to be running *away* from God. Instead of being up and at it, now, he was down and out! God let him come apart to rest awhile, before he completely came apart. He spent forty days on a run-away, not express-train, but a depressed-train whose depot would end in a deep, dark cave of gloom and doom. It seems apparent that Elijah came to the cave to die. But wait; God was not finished with Elijah. The best was yet to come!

 Have you ever descended into a cave? A dark, damp, depressing, discouraging, dirty cave of defeat? There is nothing pleasant about a cave. Our church assembly was closed for forty days from March 29, 2020, to May 10, 2020 (Mother's Day). For many, that time seemed very depressing. For my wife and I, who were experiencing some health issues and also some major disappointments, God used that time for our healing. Maybe God is doing something in your life as well. Who knows, there may be more times like these in the future for us as we move forward in our country from these pandemics. We must find God in these caves of isolation and depression.

Sometimes when difficult times come, we have a tendency to run away and head toward the wilderness. The sad thing is many Christians never make it back to the place where they once were in their service for the Lord. Take courage from Elijah's example. There is a way out of the cave!

How did Elijah get the down and outs? Let's look at his descent into the cave. 1 Kings 19:9-10 says, "And he came thither unto a cave, and lodged there; and, behold, the word of the LORD came to him, and he said unto him, What doest thou here, Elijah? And he said, I have been very jealous for the LORD God of hosts: for the children of Israel have forsaken thy covenant, thrown down thine altars, and slain thy prophets with the sword; and I, even I only, am left; and they seek my life, to take it away." No doubt, this cave was made by God, and was perhaps the cave in which He met with Moses and showed him His glory. But not just Moses; God knew down through the ages, there would be a discouraged preacher who would need this place. God prepared it for him. When we too are depressed and distraught, we must realize that God made this time, this cave, for us. Through all the events that have transpired and brought us down, God has been in control! If we feel like we're living in a cave, know that God made it just for us.

How did Elijah get into this cave? He got there because

of his diligence. He repeated this statement twice, as if God didn't know or had forgotten; "I have been very jealous for the LORD God of hosts: for the children of Israel have forsaken thy covenant, thrown down thine altars, and slain thy prophets with the sword; and I, even I only, am left; and they seek my life, to take it away" (verses 10, 14). He experienced great physical exertion. He kept going and going. So often we try to tell God, "We've been so diligent for You and Your work. Why are we in the cave?" Elijah had run 400 miles from Mount Horeb to Mount Carmel. He had journeyed forty days. He was exhausted. Sometimes, because of such physical exertion, we find ourselves absolutely exhausted. In times of exhaustion, we become vulnerable to Satan's attacks of depression and discouragement. In such times, we require rest.

Elijah not only had used great physical exertion in his ministry, but the emotional exhilaration was no doubt off the charts! Sometimes the highs and lows in ministry can seem like a roller coaster. Elijah had shut up the heavens, raised the dead, called down the fire of God; but he had also run through the barren desert. These highs and lows were more than Elijah could compensate. The high he had experienced on Mount Carmel quickly plunged to a low beneath the juniper tree. The normal, human response to the dramatic shift in emotional change is depression. I read that many MVPs of sports have severe bouts of depression after the spotlight of a great championship, such as the Super Bowl.

He also had spiritual expectations. In 1 Kings 18:36-37 we read, "And it came to pass at the time of the offering of the evening sacrifice, that Elijah the prophet came near, and said, LORD God of Abraham, Isaac, and of Israel, let it be known this day that thou art God in Israel, and that I am thy servant, and that I have done all these things at thy word. Hear me, O LORD, hear me, that this people may know that thou art the LORD God, and that thou hast turned their heart back again." We can hear the spiritual expectation in his voice. He believed a revival was going to break, that God was going to show Himself in a great and mighty way. God did show Himself mightily, but no revival came. Instead of Elijah being featured in the preacher's periodicals or written in the headlines of newspapers, he found himself on the run to no-man's land!

Elijah also found himself in this cave because of disappointments. In 1 Kings 18:36-37, we sense his disappointment in the expectation of the people. When God showed Himself, the people cried out, "The LORD, he is the God; the LORD, he is the God" (verse 39). But afterward, their hearts became indifferent. I know what it's like to have your confidence and hope in people disappointed. To believe God is going to do something great, only to see them as quick as a toddler, lose their spiritual interest. People will disappoint and let us down.

Not only was Elijah disappointed in the people, but he was disappointed in himself. 1 Kings 19:4 says, "But he himself went a day's journey into the wilderness, and came and sat down under a juniper tree: and he requested for himself that he might die; and said, It is enough; now, O LORD, take away my life; for I am not better than my fathers." No doubt he had greater expectations in his own spirituality and abilities. There are times when you do everything physically possible to be well, yet you get sick. Perhaps you practiced every financial principle you knew, and yet poverty came. God will allow circumstances to reveal our fallibilities. Paul warns us all to "have no confidence in the flesh" (Philippians 3:3).

He was disappointed in God. He spoke to God in a very impersonal manner. He referred to Him in the third person. He lost that closeness, because he had become disappointed in Him. In chapter eighteen, he prayed, "Hear me, O LORD, hear me, that this people may know <u>that thou</u> **(1st person)** art the LORD God…" (verse 37); "O LORD God shew thyself to be the God and shew everybody that I'm your man." (paraphrased). In chapter nineteen and verses 10 and 14, he said, "I have been very jealous for <u>the LORD God of hosts </u>**(3rd Person)**: for the children of Israel have forsaken thy covenant, thrown down thine altars, and slain thy prophets with the sword; and I, even I only, am left; and they seek my life, to take it away." It is almost like Elijah was ignoring God's presence. As if he was not looking God's way. Have you ever been upset with your boss and said to them, "I have worked very hard for my boss, yet my boss doesn't appreciate me!" That would be speaking to the 1st person in 3rd person. It would be a very impersonal way of speaking.

Have we ever prayed asking God for something, and when He didn't answer the way we wanted, we became disappointed in Him? We all have. We say, "Why are we in this mess? We've been serving You, unlike others. We've been so faithful. Where have You been? Why didn't You stop these circumstances from happening?" Discouragement put Elijah in the cave. "...It is enough..." he said, in verse four. He wanted to quit.

Not only disappointment, but his departure led him to the cave. Verse three says, "And when he saw that, he arose, and went for his life, and came to Beersheba, which belongeth to Judah, and left his servant there." He was the prophet. That was God's call and will for his life, his position. He also left the post, where he was serving God. There is a place that God has for every person. To leave the place, that perfect place in life where God has for you and you alone, will certainly bring depression. He not only left his position and post, but also he left his partner "...and left his servant there," (19:3). Our own failure can bring depression, but also the realization that we have failed others. The servant that Elijah left in verse 3 is never heard from again. It is apparent that this servant, who did not have the resolve of Elisha (v.19), was never heard from again. Perhaps he got out of the ministry pointing to the disappointment in the man of God he had been serving.

Desolation also brought him to the cave of depression. He began to feel as if there was no one with him. Perhaps we have allowed loneliness to put us in the cave. Maybe others have forsaken us, or death has taken those we love. I remember my dad talking about how he felt after my mom passed away. Before my mother passed, when coming into the house, Dad would always say, "Joyce, I'm home!" After she passed, he said he would still walk into the house and say, "Joyce, I'm home!" But the house was so quiet, so empty, so desolate. Dad said that after doing that several times, one day he came in, and it was as if Jesus spoke to him saying, "I'm here!" Dad said he began going into the house saying, "Jesus, I'm home!" Sometimes, desolation can put us in the deepest, darkest caves we've ever experienced. Then desolation can bring hopelessness and depression.

Now let's look at the ascent out of the cave. How did Elijah get out of the cave?

Wait On The Lord

First of all, he learned to wait on the Lord. When we feel as if we're in a cave, we must consider that the Lord is at work in us. I recently heard a sermon on a well-known verse, Isaiah 40:31. "But they that wait upon the LORD shall renew their strength; they shall mount up with wings as eagles; they shall run, and not be weary; and they shall walk, and not faint." However, this preacher pointed out the next verse, which is a continuation of the thought. How do we renew that strength? "Keep silence before me, O islands; and let the people renew their strength: let them come near; then let them speak; let us come together to judgment" (Isaiah 41:1). It may take a while, but just be still. Elijah needed rest, and God made him rest. If you are struggling with depression, you need some rest while you wait on God. Don't feel guilty when your body needs rest. Elijah slept.

Elijah not only needed rest, but also, refreshment.

God fed him. Good nourishment is needed for a healthy body and mind. Don't starve yourself during the trying times. Feed yourself with all of the nutrients that God will provide for you. We must let the Lord feed our spiritual soul as well as our body.

Not only did he gain rest and refreshment, but he received retreat. He was 400 miles away. Sometimes that is what we need, to get away from the hustle and bustle for a period of time. Jesus told his disciples after their return from a great revival excursion and upon the news of their beloved John the Baptist's execution, "And he said unto them, Come ye yourselves apart into a desert place, and rest a while: for there were many coming and going, and they had no leisure so much as to eat" (Mark 6:31). Someone has wisely said, "You had better come apart and rest awhile, or you will come apart!" Don't allow the Devil to make you feel guilty, if you need to get away for a period of time. The only caution I would give is to make sure you don't take a vacation from God.

The Word of The Lord

After Elijah learned to wait on the Lord, the Word of the Lord came unto him. When we're in the Cave of Depression, we need the Word of God to speak to our hearts. I believe this was an appearance of Christ in the Old Testament. The times that God brings us apart, unto Himself, often becomes the best times of our lives. Turn the bad news off, and turn on the Good News! Psalm 57:1 says, "Be merciful unto me, O God, be merciful unto me: for my soul trusteth in thee: yea, in the shadow of thy wings will I make my refuge, until these calamities be overpast."

The Worship of The Lord

In verses 11-13, we find the worship of God. "And he said, Go forth, and stand upon the mount before the LORD. And, behold, the LORD passed by, and a great and strong wind rent the mountains, and brake in pieces the rocks before the LORD; but the LORD was not in the wind: and after the wind an earthquake; but the LORD was not in the earthquake: And after the earthquake a fire; but the LORD was not in the fire: and after the fire a still small voice. And it was so, when Elijah heard it, that he wrapped his face in his mantle, and went out, and stood in the entering in of the cave. And, behold, there came a voice unto him, and said, What doest thou here, Elijah?" He knew he was in the holy place. He knew he was so close that he could bump into God. When we're in that time in our lives, let us wait on the Lord, let His Word speak to us, and then worship Him!

The Work of The Lord

God had a work for Elijah to do; God wasn't finished with him. In verses 15-18, God told him that he was to return, and on his way, anoint Hazael to be king over Syria, Jehu to be king over Israel, and Elisha to take his place. The ultimate victory over depression is to return to the purpose for which you were made. Work is important. Your life is important! There is work for you to do! Your life matters! Others need you: your family, your church, and your community!

Failure to get back in the fight is to flounder in pity and worthlessness. Get back to work! Realize it is not self, or anyone else for whom you are working. It is Almighty God that has called you to work for Him. You are of utmost importance to Him!

Lastly, let's look at Elijah being sent out from the cave. God told him to return. Don't allow this to be a time to get away from God. We must get on fire for Him. We must not be content to stay where we are, but go out and win others to Him. Not only return, but realize two things. Realize that His work is greater than we know. First, we don't have a monopoly on the work of God. We often think that way: "I'm the only one doing work for God." God told Elijah he still had seven thousand who hadn't bowed the knee to Baal. We're not in competition with one another. Then, realize that the work of God continues longer than we are here on this earth (verse 16). The work God commissioned Elijah to do, took three generations to complete. We, like Elijah, must realize the work of God is greater than we are and will continue after we are gone. We too can repeat the work of God and help others. 2 Timothy 2:2 says, "And the things which thou hast heard of me among many witnesses, the same commit thou to faithful men, who shall be able to teach others also." The influence of Elijah carried on for three generations of prophets. Elijah anointed Elisha (1 Kings 19:19), Elisha anointed Hazael (2 Kings 8:13), and Elisha anointed another prophet who later on anointed Jehu (2 Kings 9:1-10). Church, it's not time to hunker down. It's time to get out of the cave and be sent by God to others!

CHAPTER 8

Caveman Moses

Alone with God in the Cave of Glory

Exodus 33

The cave we are going to look at in this chapter is the same one we looked at in a previous chapter, but the occupant has changed. Earlier we looked at Elijah on Mount Horeb, but here in Exodus 33, we find it mentioned as Mount Sinai. This mount was also called "the mount of God." This is the mountain where God met face to face with Moses and gave him two tables of stone. While Moses was up on the mount with God for 40 days, the people grew restless and began to entertain themselves with the lewd pleasures of Egypt. Moses, in his anger, cast these stones to the ground and broke the commandments God had given to the people. Now, they had no Word of God. God told Moses that He would forsake the people and lead them no longer. Moses, concerned with the desperate situation, realized he needed God's help and pleaded with Him on behalf of the children of Israel. He not only pleaded for forgiveness of their sins, but he pleaded to know Him and His glory.

Exodus 32:31-33:3 "And Moses returned unto the LORD, and said, Oh, this people have sinned a great sin, and have made them gods of gold. Yet now, if thou wilt forgive their sin and if not, blot me, I pray thee, out of thy book which thou hast written. And the LORD said unto Moses, Whosoever hath sinned against me, him will I blot out of my book. Therefore now go, lead the people unto the place of which I have spoken unto thee: behold, mine Angel shall go before thee: nevertheless in the day when I visit I will visit their sin upon them. And the LORD plagued the people, because they made the calf, which Aaron made. And the LORD said unto Moses, Depart, and go up hence, thou and the people which thou hast brought up out of the land of Egypt, unto the land which I sware unto Abraham, to Isaac, and to Jacob, saying, Unto thy seed will I give it: And I will send an angel before thee; and I will drive out the Canaanite, the Amorite, and the Hittite, and the Perizzite, the Hivite, and the Jebusite: Unto a land flowing with milk and honey: for I will not go up in the midst of thee; for thou art a stiffnecked people: lest I consume thee in the way."

God told Moses to depart. He told him that He would send an angel to go with them, but they would have to go without God Himself. But Moses was not satisfied with God's answer. Sadly, most Christians are satisfied with an angel of the Lord rather than desiring the presence of God. We need more than God's help; we need God!

Moses put up a tabernacle, "the Tabernacle of the congregation" (Exodus 33:7-10). This was not the tabernacle that they would make in a few months, but just a tent that he pitched. Moses goes in and meets with God.

"And the LORD spake unto Moses face to face, as a man speaketh unto his friend. And he turned again into the camp: but his servant Joshua, the son of Nun, a young man, departed not out of the tabernacle. And Moses said unto the LORD, See, thou sayest unto me, Bring up this people: and thou hast not let me know whom thou wilt send with me. Yet thou hast said, I know thee by name, and thou hast also found grace in my sight. Now therefore, I pray thee, if I have found grace in thy sight, shew me now thy way, that I may know thee, that I may find grace in thy sight: and consider that this nation is thy people. And he said, My presence shall go with thee, and I will give thee rest. And he said unto him, If thy presence go not with me, carry us not up hence. For wherein shall it be known here that I and thy people have found grace in thy sight? is it not in that thou goest with us? so shall we be separated, I and thy people, from all the people that are upon the face of the earth. And the LORD said unto Moses, I will do this thing also that thou hast spoken: for thou hast found grace in my sight, and I know thee by name. And he said, I beseech thee, shew me thy glory. And he said, I will make all my goodness pass before thee, and I will proclaim the name of the LORD before thee; and will be gracious to whom I will be gracious, and will shew mercy on whom I will shew mercy" (Exodus 33:11-19).

What separates God's people from everyone else? God's presence and His glory. What happens when we are not conscious of the presence of God in our midst? There is no separation, no distinction between us and the rest of this world. We can get in the presence of God in the same real way that Moses did, but we can't expect to get there on our own terms. God had certain requirements for Moses:

"And the LORD said unto Moses, Hew thee two tables of stone like unto the first: and I will write upon these tables the words that were in the first tables, which thou brakest. And be ready in the morning, and come up in the morning unto mount Sinai, and present thyself there to me in the top of the mount. And no man shall come up with thee, neither let any man be seen throughout all the mount; neither let the flocks nor herds feed before that mount. And he hewed two tables of stone like unto the first; and Moses rose up early in the morning, and went up unto mount Sinai, as the LORD had commanded him, and took in his hand the two tables of stone" (Exodus 34:1-4).

So how did Moses experience the glory of God in the cave? First, he sought the Lord. He sought God's way (Exodus 33:13), God's glory (verse 18), and God's presence (verse 15). Do we desire to see God? Do we seek Him, desiring that He go with us each step that we take? Do we get alone with God, putting away all the other distractions in order to truly seek Him?

Secondly, he stood with God (Exodus 33:21 & 34:5). If we are going to get ahold of God, we must determine to take a stand (Ephesians. 6:10-14). We are challenged to withstand, but we will never withstand, unless we are standing clothed and dependent upon His armour. When Moses stood with God, then God stood with him. When we stand on our own terms in our own place, we will have the uneasy feeling that God is not with us. But if we stand with God, He won't make us stand alone. There is no fear when we stand with God!

Thirdly, he stayed. He was on the mount for forty days. We want instant service, but God did not show His glory to Moses until he had stayed awhile. We must be "steadfast, unmoveable, always abounding in the work of the Lord" (1 Corinthians 15:58). If we'll be persistent, God will reveal Himself to us. So many of us are content to just get a little taste of God, but not Moses. He didn't abandon His presence.

God showed him. He showed Moses His goodness. His goodness is who He is. Most Christians don't ever get close enough to God to really see and enjoy His goodness. If they did, they wouldn't complain and be so dissatisfied. They wouldn't bicker so much. Then, God showed him His grace. His grace is what He does. Most people don't get far enough from the mercy of God to experience the grace of God. But God not only desires to show us mercy; He desires to show us His grace: His blessing, His unmerited favor. Lastly, he showed him His glory. His glory is what illuminates. He reveals His presence and His holiness that removes all doubt.

Then Moses stooped before Him in worship (Exodus 34:8). If we want to get a hold of God, we must humble ourselves before Him. Isaiah 57:15 says, "For thus saith the high and lofty One that inhabiteth eternity, whose name is Holy; I dwell in the high and holy place, with him also that is of a contrite and humble spirit, to revive the spirit of the humble, and to revive the heart of the contrite ones."

He sacrificed. What did God ask him to bring? He asked for two new stones to be hewn (Exodus 34:1). God had made the first two, but this time God asked him to bring them. Don't come to God expecting something without having a willingness to give something. Exodus 34:20 says, "And none shall appear before me empty." What did God do with his offering? God took those two tables of stone, which represented the heart of man, and wrote the Word of God upon them (2 Corinthians 3:3). He blessed them, just like He will take our offering and bless it. He'll make more out of it, if we will just bring it to Him.

God sustained him. He gave him His Word in Exodus 34:28, "And he was there with the LORD forty days and forty nights; he did neither eat bread, nor drink water. And he wrote upon the tables the words of the covenant, the ten commandments." Then, God gave him His likeness. When Moses came down off the mount, "the skin of his face shone while he talked with him" (Exodus 34:29). He not only had the Word of God in his hand, but the smile of God on his face. Can others tell when we have God in our lives? Not only did God give Moses His Word and His likeness, but He sustained his needs. God is willing to supply all our needs (Philippians 4:19). When we get the Lord, we have all we need!

Moses got in the glory in the cave; the glory got on him; and when he came down from the mount, he made a difference for his people.

CHAPTER 9

Caveman Obadiah

The Caves of Refuge

1 Kings 18

In this passage, we're going to look at some difficult times. The children of Israel had forsaken God. The northern kingdom separated and followed idolatry, as did the pagan nations around them. They had a very wicked king "which did sell himself to work wickedness" (1 Kings 21:25); that king was Ahab. His wife, Jezebel, made his wickedness even greater. Elijah, the man of God, prophesied against them and preached a message of repentance. Sometimes God, in order to get people's attention, allows difficult circumstances to come to a nation.

Elijah prophesied that it would not rain for three years. He prayed, and God shut the windows of heaven. God hid Elijah as famine swept through the land. Unable to find him, Jezebel took her anger out on the other prophets and slew them with a vengeance.

God finally tells Elijah, that it's time to come out of hiding. "And it came to pass after many days, that the word of the LORD came to Elijah in the third year, saying, Go, shew thyself unto Ahab; and I will send rain upon the earth. And Elijah went to shew himself unto Ahab. And there was a sore famine in Samaria. And Ahab called Obadiah, which was the governor of his house. (Now Obadiah feared the LORD greatly:

For it was so, when Jezebel cut off the prophets of the LORD, that Obadiah took an hundred prophets, and hid them by fifty in a cave, and fed them with bread and water.) And Ahab said unto Obadiah, Go into the land, unto all fountains of water, and unto all brooks: peradventure we may find grass to save the horses and mules alive, that we lose not all the beasts. So they divided the land between them to pass throughout it: Ahab went one way by himself, and Obadiah went another way by himself. And as Obadiah was in the way, behold, Elijah met him: and he knew him, and fell on his face, and said, Art thou that my lord Elijah? And he answered him, I am: go, tell thy lord, Behold, Elijah is here" (1 Kings 18:1-8).

Let's first consider the dwellers in these two caves of refuge. They were saved. The Lord had put them in this place of safety. John 10:27-29 promises us a place of safety and salvation: "My sheep hear my voice, and I know them, and they follow me: And I give unto them eternal life; and they shall never perish, neither shall any man pluck them out of my hand. My Father, which gave them me, is greater than all; and no man is able to pluck them out of my Father's hand."

They not only had salvation, but they had an adversary. Just as Ahab and Jezebel were out to seek the lives of these prophets, we too have an adversary. 1 Peter 5:8 commands us to "Be sober, be vigilant; because your adversary the devil, as a roaring lion, walketh about, seeking whom he may devour." He's looking for those whose lives he can destroy. In Revelation 9:11, he is called Apollyon, which means "destroyer." But in God, we have a place of security, as these prophets found security from their enemies in these caves.

Then let us consider these two caves. They are a type of Jesus Christ. In Him, we are secure; safe from sin and death. "Jesus said unto her, I am the resurrection, and the life: he that believeth in me, though he were dead, yet shall he live: And whosoever liveth and believeth in me shall never die. Believest thou this?" (John 11:25-26). They are also a type of the church: a place of refuge from this world. The church is a place where we can, as Jesus said, "come...apart...and rest a while" (Mark 6:31). It's where someone who has been saved can come to be ministered to and grow in the Lord.

What do these caves provide? First, they provide salvation (Romans 10:9-10). They provide security. No one, not even yourself, can pluck you out of God's hand (John 10:27-29). They provide safety. Come to the point where you can say, "I'm just going to trust God for my safety." Hebrews 13:5-6 says, "Let your conversation be without covetousness; and be content with such things as ye have: for he hath said, I will never leave thee, nor forsake thee. So that we may boldly say, The Lord is my helper, and I will not fear what man shall do unto me." Then they provide separation. They were separated from the world and those who would try to bring them harm. In 2 Corinthians 6:14-17 we read, "Be ye not unequally yoked together with unbelievers: for what fellowship hath righteousness with unrighteousness? and what communion hath light with darkness? And what concord hath Christ with Belial? or what part hath he that believeth with an infidel? And what agreement hath the temple of God with idols? for ye are the temple of the living God; as God hath said, I will dwell in them, and walk in them; and I will be their God, and they shall be my people. Wherefore come out from among them, and be ye separate, saith the Lord, and touch not the unclean thing; and I will receive you." Then we see the supply. Obadiah supplied them with bread and water throughout this time of famine (1 Kings 18:13). You may think, "What are we going to do, if the economy fails?" Let's serve God. Let's trust God. Let's just keep on living for God (Psalm 37:25). Philippians 4:19 promises, "But my God shall supply all your need according to his riches in glory by Christ Jesus." God has obligated Himself, as we live for Him, to bankrupt Heaven before He will allow our needs to be unsupplied.

Why were these men in the cave? Because Obadiah, whose name means "servant of Jehovah," had a cause (Proverbs 29:18). He was working for an ungodly king, yet he was known for his testimony. You may work for an ungodly employer, yet you can maintain a godly testimony and faith. God allowed Obadiah to have an influential part in opening up and bringing salvation to the nation of Israel. Not only did he save these prophets, but in doing so, he helped save the king and the entire kingdom from an invasion by the king of Assyria (1 Kings 20:13, 28, 35; 22:8). All because he realized, there was a cause. What is the cause for your life (1 Samuel 17:29)? In order to bring people to the caves of refuge, to be the soul winners that we ought to, there must come a point in time where we say, "There is a cause!"

Compassion brought about Obadiah's obedience to the cause. Jude 1:22-23 commands us, "And of some have compassion, making a difference: And others save with fear, pulling them out of the fire; hating even the garment spotted by the flesh." We must see the condition of our world and be concerned for the needs of others.

Obadiah was nervous and didn't feel courageous (1 Kings 18:9-14), but God used him. He used him, because he was meek and humble. We must choose to take courage, even when fearful and afraid. Don't look at your hands, at your muscles to see how strong you are. The key to courage is found in Ephesians 6:10, "Finally, my brethren, be strong in the Lord, and in the power of his might." Courage comes from knowing that God is able, that He can do anything! He can use anyone! Paul said, "I can do all things through Christ which strengtheneth me" (Philippians 4:13). Don't look to your abilities, your talents, or how many are standing with you; look to the Lord.

When Obadiah brought the prophets to the cave, it was during a time of famine. He took care of them by providing them with bread and water. We need to have care for others. We must give of ourselves and become caretakers, like the Samaritan found in Luke 10. We don't need to be selfish, stingy Christians. Let's continually give of ourselves. It's not even enough to just bring someone to Christ; we must get them into church, help them follow the Lord, and encourage them in their faith.

There was a cost involved for Obadiah (1 Kings 18:4, 13). Serving God takes some sacrifice. Obadiah wasn't looking out for himself, but looking to the needs of these prophets.

Obadiah may not have felt like he accomplished much for the Lord, but no doubt there were many who, when he got to Heaven, thanked him for saving their lives by being willing to obey the task he was given. You may feel like the most insignificant person around, but God will use anyone who is willing to let Him have his life. Will you help bring others to the caves of refuge?

CHAPTER 10

Caveman Lot

The Cave of Degradation
Genesis 19

All caves are not equal. There are caves that are illumined like jeweled caverns with the glory of God. Moses was placed, in such a cave, by The Holy and Omnipotent One. When he came out, his face glowed with the glory of God. Then there are deep, dark caves which vex the souls of their spiritual inhabitants. They become destitute, abandoned, and void of the glorious light of God.

The Cave that Lot descended into was a far cry from the blessed abode that he had enjoyed years prior with Uncle Abe! Abraham's old-fashioned walk in the land of blessings, with the presence of God, was much too old-fashioned for Lot. Being a pilgrim and stranger in a world filled with alluring temptations and opportunities for promotions and advancement, did not appeal to a man like Lot. His ambitions lured him to Sodom, a low-land of worldly living, yet a place with the promise of lofty positions in the gates of politics, business, and pleasure.

The sparkle of city lights gleamed in the eyes of his wife. Lot's daughters would have the opportunity to enjoy the finer things in life and partake of the best entertainment that the world of Sodom could offer.

Though Lot and his family reached the pinnacle of success in the low-land of Sodom living, the remnant of Lot and his family descended into the depths of "The Cave of Degradation" in the high ground of deliverance.

I am concerned for the many Christians who have gotten too accustomed to their caves during this "pandemic" and have not found their way back to the House of God. Caves are temporary and never intended as a place of departure from the will of God. Too long in a cave, out of the will of God, is a recipe for disaster, as it was for Lot.

During this time of "pandemic," God may be bringing us close to Himself in caves of separation. However, all the caves of the Bible were temporary in purpose and intended for strengthening the believer in faith and reliance upon God. Otherwise, the caves may have become an inescapable dungeon or grave!

Peter uses Lot as the example for the believer in times of trials and temptations, to rely upon God's deliverance from impending loss and destruction. We must not be like Lot, who chose his own will and suffered the vexation and loss of everything.

II Peter 2:4-9 says, "For if God spared not the angels that sinned, but cast them down to hell, and delivered them into chains of darkness, to be reserved unto judgment; And spared not the old world, but saved Noah the eighth person, a preacher of righteousness, bringing in the flood upon the world of the ungodly; And turning the cities of Sodom and Gomorrha into ashes condemned them with an overthrow, making them an ensample unto those that after should live ungodly; And delivered just Lot, vexed with the filthy conversation of the wicked: (For that righteous man dwelling among them, in seeing and hearing, vexed his righteous soul from day to day with their unlawful deeds;) The Lord knoweth how to deliver the godly out of temptations, and to reserve the unjust unto the day of judgment to be punished:"

Of all of the caves and cavemen that we have considered, Lot and his cave of degradation is the worst cave of all.

Let's consider:
The Degradation of the Cave

What happened in the life of Lot and his family that brought them from the land flowing with milk and honey, the sparkling lights of Sodom, to the dark, low-living Cave of Degradation?

First of all, there had not been enough contrasting distinction from the inside to the outside of the home. When the angels came to warn Lot they preferred dwelling in the street rather than within the walls of Lot's house. Lot's house had become too much like Sodom.

Genesis 19:2 says, "And he said, Behold now, my lords, turn in, I pray you, into your servant's house, and tarry all night, and wash your feet, and ye shall rise up early, and go on your ways. And they said, Nay; but we will abide in the street all night."

Secondly, there were no convictions or standards for his family. He had become in-laws with outlaws of Sodom. His children had learned the way of the heathen and

Lot's social drinking led him to become a sot drunkard in a depraved cave.

In 2 Corinthians 6:14 the Bible teaches us, "Be ye not unequally yoked together with unbelievers: for what fellowship hath righteousness with unrighteousness? and what communion hath light with darkness?"

Thirdly, there was no concern for the spiritual well-being of his family. Lot cared more for his social standing with the Sodomites than the spiritual or physical well-being of his daughters. He offered his daughters to the perverts that sought harm to the angels. "And have no fellowship with the unfruitful works of darkness, but rather reprove them" (Ephesians 5:11).

A Little Leaven
'Twas not a lot but just a little,
'twas not a dot but just a tittle.
But 'twas too much. That little leaven,
That grew too much, and filled the oven!
It filled the stove and spoiled the floors.
It filled the house and ran out the doors!
It grew so much I soon discovered,
I could not hide nor keep it covered!

'Twas not that much, but just a tad,
Of beer and wine that ruined the lad.
'Twas not a lot, but just a tot,
That turned the tot into a sot!
A social drink to give some spunk,
 that turned the spunk into a drunk!
A word to the wise should be enough.
A little leaven is way too much!
by: Lonnie Moore

Lot's condescension to low living had a terrible price. Sodom and Gomorrah began all over again in this Cave of Degradation. There are no guarantees for Sodom and Gomorrah living.

The Descent into the Cave
Genesis 13

The descent into the depths of his lowly cave was not a rapid descent, but rather a gradual decline. As I see it, there were six downward steps from the lofty heights of Hebron to his lowly dungeon of depravity found in Chapters 13-14 of Genesis.

Step 1 - Leaving the land of promises (13:9).
The same is true for Christians when they begin to forget the promise of blessings in God's Word. When he left the Land of Promise, he left the godly influence on his children and family of the man of God and the safety of dwelling in the midst of God's people. The same is true when a Christian forsakes the House of God (Hebrews 10:25).

Step 2 - Looking to the land of pleasures (13:10).
The land was good grazing for cattle but a spiritual desert for the family. It is better to not look when the look is in the wrong direction. It was the look that tempted Achan to take the forbidden, which cost him everything including he and his family's life.

Step 3 - Longing and pursuing ever closer to the land of prosperity (13:10-11).
He developed a lust for a land which was godless as he kept moving ever closer.

Step 4 - Living in the land of perversity (13:12-13).
He seemed justified by the prosperity he and his family

enjoyed with the success of the suburbs of Sodom. Many wayward children of God soothe their conscience by the success of worldly living. However, success is temporary and the losses soon to be experienced, are eternal.

Step 5 - Losing but not learning (Genesis 14).
Lot lost everything and was taken captive with the Sodomites. Abraham and his servants rescued Lot and retrieved all that was lost. The King of Sodom offered to reward Abraham, but Abraham refused and dedicated everything to Melchizedek, the King of Salem. It appears that Lot, who should have learned a valuable lesson, took the offer from the King of Sodom and returned, was made a judge, and dwelled in the gate of Sodom.

Step 6 - Lingering in Sodom (Genesis 19).
Perhaps Lot had great intentions of leaving Sodom someday, but he lingered for more great opportunities. It might have been the great advancement in the Government of Sodom that the King of Sodom had offered to Abraham. It could have been that Lot intended to stay and recoup some of the financial losses he had incurred. Perhaps it was his daughters who refused to leave their friends and potential suitors, or his wife who had become entrenched in the society of Sodom. Whatever the cause, It would have been best for Lot to cut his losses and save his family. Yet, he lingered and lost everything.

Step 7 - Lamenting instead of repenting (Genesis 19).
Lot lamented his losses instead of repenting and heeding the warning. He perhaps could have saved his wife had he taken to the high ground of which the angels bid

him. However, he longed for a little of the old life with the little cities and lost his wife. He descended into the cave instead.

The decisions made by Lot and his family were foolish.

Lot made the horrid decision to pursue worldly ambitions, compromise his convictions, abandon his covenant with the godly, while yoking with the most godless of Sodom. Consider the names of the Kings with whom Lot had aligned and allied himself. (14:2)

- Bera, "Son of Evil," the king of Sodom
- Bersha, "with Iniquity or Wickedness," king of Gomorrah
- Shinab, "Splendour of the Father," king of Admah
- Shemeber "Illustrious," king of Zeboiim
- King of Bela "Destruction"

Though all of these kings were alluring with such promising vanities, Lot should have known by their names and the fruit of their doings that he had no reason to be unequally yoked with such unbelievers. No doubt, Lot was convinced that he could remain true to Jehovah and enjoy his sins for a season. Many, like Lot, have made a deal with the Devil for pride, pleasure, or prosperity only to be deceived and lose everything. There are no guarantees when departing from the faith to make a safe return. These many years in the ministry, I have witnessed many casualties. I have warned fathers when backsliding, you may return and make it back to the church, but there is no guarantee that your family will. How true this was for Lot!

Lot's wife made the horrid decision to turn back. Why?

Maybe it was for her family, possessions, positions, pleasures, or perhaps natural instincts. For too long, she had habitually walked by sight and not by faith. She was unsubmissive to the Word of God. She had failed to teach her daughters to be virtuous. Jesus has warned each of us to, "Remember Lot's wife." She became a pillar of salt, a testimony of the consequence of vanity. "There is a way that seemeth right unto a man, but the end thereof are the ways of death" (Proverbs 16:25).

The decision of Lot's sons-in-law to scoff at the warning of judgment was of eternal consequence. Jesus warns in Matthew 7:13, "Enter ye in at the strait gate: for wide is the gate, and broad is the way, that leadeth to destruction, and many there be which go in thereat." There is no promise of tomorrow. 2 Corinthians 6:2 warns, "behold, now is the accepted time; behold, now is the day of salvation."

Lot's daughters made the hasty decision to not wait on God's choices for their lives, but rather settle for a perverted alternative which marked their offspring for generations. God's will and choices for our lives is always best. We must wait on the Lord. "Trust in the LORD with all thine heart; and lean not unto thine own understanding. In all thy ways acknowledge him, and he shall direct thy paths" (Proverbs 3:5).

The Dismay of the Cave

He loved that which could not or would not love him. His love was, like Demas, for this present world. 2 Timothy 4:10 says, "For Demas hath forsaken me, having loved this present world, and is departed unto Thessalonica; Crescens to Galatia, Titus unto Dalmatia."

He had loved the world and left the love of the Father. He had been seduced by the world's evil trinity, "the lust of the flesh, and the lust of the eyes, and the pride of life" (I John 2:16). God's Word warns us in 1 John 2:15, "Love not the world, neither the things that are in the world. If any man love the world, the love of the Father is not in him. For all that is in the world, the lust of the flesh, and the lust of the eyes, and the pride of life, is not of the Father, but is of the world."

Where was his learning found? (14:12-16) He did not learn from wise old Uncle Abe, but was schooled by the heathen who "professing themselves to be wise, they became fools" (Romans 1:22). It seems that Lot and all of his clan were top of their class in the school of the heathen. However, it is a school for fools! "Thus saith the LORD, Learn not the way of the heathen, and be not dismayed at the signs of heaven; for the heathen are dismayed at them" (Jeremiah 10:2).

We are instructed to become a fool in this world that we may become wise. 1 Corinthians 3:18 tells us, "Let no man deceive himself. If any man among you seemeth to be wise in this world, let him become a fool, that he may be wise. What was his loss? He lost everything but his salvation. He lost his position at the gate, the possessions he had accumulated in Sodom, and his family. He totally lost his way.

The Deliverance from the Cave

God is a merciful God. He would not leave Lot to perish with the heathen. God has provided a higher ground even for the backslider (verse 17). If you have found yourself, as Lot, "vexed by the filthy conversation of the wicked," then take the high ground and forsake the low land of living. God is a prayer-hearing, prayer-answering God.

"And turning the cities of Sodom and Gomorrah into ashes condemned them with an overthrow, making them an ensample unto those that after should live ungodly; and delivered just Lot, vexed with the filthy conversation of the wicked: (For that righteous man dwelling among them, in seeing and hearing, vexed his righteous soul from day to day with their unlawful deeds;) the Lord knoweth how to deliver the godly out of temptations, and to reserve the unjust unto the day of judgment to be punished" (2 Peter 2:6-9).

Lot did not accept the offer by the angels for higher ground, and he lost his wife. Perhaps if she had been on higher ground rather than the low-land vicinity of Sodom in Zoar ("Insignificance") she would not have turned back and been overcome with the destruction of Sodom! But, she would not have this "insignificance." She would not settle for less than magnificence! She would not be submissive! She had to salvage a portion of her old life. There have been many men who have lost their wives to "this present evil world," because they chose to settle too close to the condemned places, reserved for destruction.

I believe it was Spurgeon who said, "If it were not for the awful destruction and judgment outside of the ark, Noah could not have endured the stench inside the ark!"

CHAPTER 11
The Caves of Delusion

I would rather be in the battle with Jesus than be in the cave without Him!

In 1 Samuel 13:5-6 we read, "And the Philistines gathered themselves together to fight with Israel, thirty thousand chariots, and six thousand horsemen, and people as the sand which is on the sea shore in multitude: and they came up, and pitched in Michmash, eastward from Bethaven. When the men of Israel saw that they were in a strait, (for the people were distressed,) then the people did hide themselves in caves, and in thickets, and in rocks, and in high places, and in pits."

Sometimes we are put in the cave by God. When God puts us in the cave, just as He was with Moses, He is with us in the cave. If we learn to respond to Him, we will come out of the cave with the power of God and His countenance upon us. The times when God places us in the cave are often not circumstances of our choosing, but are there to teach and train us, as was the case with David and his men. However, if we choose by convenience to flee to the caves to hide rather than face our problems without God putting us there, we will be in the cave without Him. We will be delusional. There we will abide fearing, without knowing Divine direction or guidance. In this passage, we see that the children of Israel had become accustomed to hiding in caves rather than standing and defending their God-given lands.

How did these descendants of more than conquerors, blessed with the greatest heritage on earth, forsake their fields of harvest and vineyards of Eschol to flee to the barren, dark caves?

The Spirituality of the People became Diminished.

- They desired a king instead of God to rule them.

They sought a king to serve, rather than God, to be their confidence and trust. (1 Samuel 12:12-15, "And when ye saw that Nahash the king of the children of Ammon came against you, ye said unto me, Nay; but a king shall reign over us: when the LORD your God was your king. Now therefore behold the king whom ye have chosen, and whom ye have desired! and, behold, the LORD hath set a king over you. If ye will fear the LORD, and serve him, and obey his voice, and not rebel against the commandment of the LORD, then shall both ye and also the king that reigneth over you continue following the LORD your God: But if ye will not obey the voice of the LORD, but rebel against the commandment of the LORD, then shall the hand of the LORD be against you, as it was against your fathers.")

They sought a man to be held to God's high standard; while in their own lives, they were satisfied with "a form of godliness, but denying the power thereof..." (2 Timothy 3:5). We cannot simply rely upon others in authority to do right for us, we must choose to do right ourselves.

- They became confident in their own flesh.

They were confident in their own flesh. God had given Saul a victory over the Ammonites (chapter 12), and now with only two swords (1 Samuel 13:22), he was ready to take on the Philistines, the makers of swords. We cannot take on anyone in our own power. "For though we walk in the flesh, we do not war after the flesh: (For the weapons of our warfare are not carnal, but mighty through God to the pulling down of strong holds;) Casting down imaginations, and every high thing that exalteth itself against the knowledge of God, and bringing into captivity every thought to the obedience of Christ; And having in a readiness to revenge all disobedience, when your obedience is fulfilled" (2 Corinthians 10:3-6). We cannot match sword for sword with our enemies. They are far greater than us. If we try to use their weapons, we will lose this battle. Take courage, ye men of faith! Through Christ, we have mightier weapons than they.

- They forgot the great things God had done for them.

Not only were they seeking a fleshly king, satisfied with their form of godliness, and confident in their own strength, but they had forgotten the great things God had done for them. In 1 Samuel 12:24-25, Samuel commanded the people, "Only fear the LORD, and serve him in truth with all your heart: for consider how great things he hath done for you. But if ye shall still do wickedly, ye shall be consumed, both ye and your king." Have we forgotten the things that God has done for us?

- They walked by sight rather than by faith.

They saw the enemy and fled to the cave. We must quit fearing what man can do and trust what God can do. 2 Corinthians 5:7-10 says, "(For we walk by faith, not by sight:) We are confident, I say, and willing rather to be absent from the body, and to be present with the Lord. Wherefore we labour, that, whether present or absent, we may be accepted of him. For we must all appear before the judgment seat of Christ; that every one may receive the things done in his body, according to that he hath done, whether it be good or bad." We don't have to fight; we just have to stand. The Bible commands us to "...Resist the devil, and he will flee from you" (James 4:7). The word resist literally means "to take a stand." The admonition we have from the New Testament is to take a stand and allow God to do the fighting for us.

The carnality of the people became dominant.

"Now there was no smith found throughout all the land of Israel: for the Philistines said, Lest the Hebrews make them swords or spears: But all the Israelites went down to the Philistines, to sharpen every man his share, and his coulter, and his axe, and his mattock. Yet they had a file for the mattocks, and for the coulters, and for the forks, and for the axes, and to sharpen the goads. So it came to pass in the day of battle, that there was neither sword nor spear found in the hand of any of the people that were with Saul and Jonathan: but with Saul and with Jonathan his son was there found. And the garrison of the Philistines went out to the passage of Michmash" (1 Samuel 13:19-23).

The "garrison" was their headquarters or authority of the land. The children of Israel had allowed the Philistines to become their authority. It seems in America today, we have subjected ourselves to the authority of those who are heathen and do not believe in God. The Philistines told the children of Israel that they did not have a need for swords, but rather they should concern themselves with making a living. The Philistines provided them with farming implements to plow, sow, and cultivate their lands for food, with the evil intent of later, reaping the harvest with their swords.

They traded their weapons for mattocks.

2 Corinthians 10:3-6 says, "For though we walk in the flesh, we do not war after the flesh: (For the weapons of our warfare are not carnal, but mighty through God to the pulling down of strong holds;) Casting down imaginations, and every high thing that exalteth itself against the knowledge of God, and bringing into captivity every thought to the obedience of Christ; And having in a readiness to revenge all disobedience, when your obedience is fulfilled."

Consider our mighty weapons which we have laid aside, capable of conquering evil forces invading our land?

First, we have lost the fervent weapon of prayer. Prayer is seeking the Divine favor of an Omniscient, Omnipotent, and Omnipresent God: our Creator. He has been shunned and traded for the wisdom of this world and the how to's of success in this present world. Jeremiah 33:2-3 tells us, "Thus saith the LORD the maker thereof, the LORD that formed it, to establish it; the LORD is his name; Call unto me, and I will answer thee, and shew thee great and mighty things, which thou knowest not."

Second, we have laid aside the most formidable weapon: the Word of God. It's description is given to us in Hebrews 4:12. "For the word of God is quick, and powerful, and sharper than any twoedged sword, piercing even to the dividing asunder of soul and spirit, and of the joints and marrow, and is a discerner of the thoughts and intents of the heart." We have laid it aside, only to pick up "…every man his share, and his coulter, and his axe, and his mattock." Paul again admonished Timothy in 2 Timothy 2:4, "No man that warreth entangleth himself with the affairs of this life; that he may please him who hath chosen him to be a soldier."

The third great weapon of the Christian soldier is faith. Jesus said that faith, even the size of a mustard seed, could move mountains. Matthew 17:20 says, "And Jesus said unto them, … If ye have faith as a grain of mustard seed, ye shall say unto this mountain, Remove hence to yonder place; and it shall remove; and nothing shall be impossible unto you."

When our interest becomes more about the prosperity of our havens and less about preserving our heritage, there will come a day that we will lose both. **They abandoned their smiths for the ungodly smiths who would destroy them.**

Who are the Smiths that have been lost in our nation? First and foremost are the preachers. Those men of God who take the Sword of the Word of God and teach us how to use it. They have been traded away for the intelligentsia of this world, those who do not know and cannot proclaim God's Word. Paul admonished Timothy to train "smiths." "And the things that thou hast heard of me among many witnesses, the same commit thou to faithful men, who shall be able to teach others also. Thou therefore endure hardness, as a good soldier of Jesus Christ. No man that warreth entangleth himself with the affairs of this life; that he may please him who hath chosen him to be a soldier" (2 Timothy 2:2-4).

Not only have the preachers been traded away, but the assembly "the church" has as well. The church is the smith's shop where the fire of God is hot and the iron is forged and hammered into mighty weapons for God. Hebrews 10:24-25 commands us, "And let us consider one another to provoke unto love and to good works: Not forsaking the assembling of ourselves together, as the manner of some is; but exhorting one another: and so much the more, as ye see the day approaching." We need to be in church. Why? To help, encourage, and sharpen one another (Proverbs 27:17). The church has been removed from its foundation, and its purpose has been lost. It has been replaced by entertainment and toy making. The once despised, hot, smelly smith shop, has been replaced by the ornate entertainment centers, sports arenas, and banqueting halls.

Thirdly, and not least of all, we have grieved the greatest Smith of all, the Holy Spirit! We have forsaken our devotion time with the Holy Spirit of God. We must daily spend time in the "Smithing School" of the Holy Spirit, allowing Him to equip us to be the soldier that we need to be for Him. (Ephesians 6:10-17, "Finally, my brethren, be strong in the Lord, and in the power of his might. Put on the whole armour of God, that ye may be able to stand against the wiles of the devil. For we wrestle not against flesh and blood, but against principalities, against powers, against the rulers of the darkness of this world, against spiritual wickedness in high places. Wherefore take unto you the whole armour of God, that ye may be able to withstand in the evil day, and having done all, to stand. Stand therefore, having your loins girt about with truth, and having on the breastplate of righteousness; And your feet shod with the preparation of the gospel of peace; Above all, taking the shield of faith, wherewith ye shall be able to quench all the fiery darts of the wicked. And take the helmet of salvation, and the sword of the Spirit, which is the word of God:")

In their carnality, the children of Israel not only traded their weapons and smiths, but they lost touch with God. They caused God to become silent. In chapter thirteen, when Saul couldn't get God to answer, he tried to force his own will. He made his own sacrifice in order to rally the people around himself. But Samuel told him that his decision was foolish and that God would replace him with a man after His own heart. Because of his actions, Saul lost it all. If we do not know God's will, we had better stand still. If we are in the dark, we need to wait for God to shed His light on the way He wants us to go.

Because they felt powerless in their situation without God, they turned to the caves and isolated themselves. They felt the best they could do was try to survive alone, but God has never worked that way. The devil will try to make us feel like we are all alone in the battle, but that isn't the case.

So how did they get out of the cave and possess the land again? First, they had to have faith in God. Jonathan said in 1 Samuel 14:1, "Come, and let us go over to the Philistines' garrison, that is on the other side" And in verse six, he told his armour bearer, "...it may be that the LORD will work for us: for there is no restraint to the

LORD to save by many or by few." They chose to have faith in God in order to do something great for God. (Daniel 11:32, ".. .but the people that do know their God shall be strong, and do exploits.") And they asked God for a sign. They decided to show themselves to the Philistines. If the Philistines told them to come up to them, they would go up; but if they told them that they would come down to them, they would wait for them to come down, because God was going to deliver them into their hand. Either way, they would be the winners. We must be willing to trust God, as Jonathan and his armor bearer did, and venture out of our comfort zones. Oh, that we could say, "Lord, here's my life; see what You can do with it."

They were willing to accept difficulties. Jonathan and his armor bearer were in a canyon and the scoffing Philistines had the high ground. We find them, in verse 4, "Between a rock and a hard place." One rock was named Bozez ("shining rock" perhaps marble), and the other was named Senah ("thorny cliff"). Yet, even in this difficult situation, he climbed up with his hands and feet (verse 13).

Perhaps you are in a financial cave of bad decisions, and you want out. What must you do? You must be willing to overcome the difficulties, face the creditors, do without some comforts, persevere, climb hand over feet like Jonathan, and get to higher ground.

Perhaps you want out of a deep, dark cave of addiction, or perhaps a health issue is requiring you to lose excessive weight or drastically change your diet. Jonathan went, perhaps for days, without food. It will not be easy, but you must be willing to accept the difficulties. Trust

God to help you begin the climb up the thorny cliff, out of the canyon of low-living and reach the summit of God's will for your life.

Regardless of the cave you are in, the devil will make it difficult to overcome. You must accept difficulty before you will accept the success of the summit.

They chose to go alone; they did not proclaim for all to hear what they were going to do. Jonathan was misunderstood and rejected by his own father. When the battle was being won, the rest of the people did not realize that it was Jonathan who had fought. Saul made a crazy decision and said that anyone who ate before he received glory for the victory would be put to death. We must choose to be willing to walk alone and be misunderstood even by our own family at times. But if we give God all the glory, He will give us the victory. "So the LORD saved Israel that day: and the battle passed over unto Bethaven" (1 Samuel 14:23).

CHAPTER 12

Caveman Gideon

It is Time to Get Out of the Cave!

Judges 6:1-6

"And the children of Israel did evil in the sight of the LORD: and the LORD delivered them into the hand of Midian seven years. And the hand of Midian prevailed against Israel: and because of the Midianites **the children of Israel made them the dens which are in the mountains, and caves, and strong holds.** And so it was, when Israel had sown, that the Midianites came up, and the Amalekites, and the children of the east, even they came up against them; And they encamped against them, and destroyed the increase of the earth, till thou come unto Gaza, and left no sustenance for Israel, neither sheep, nor ox, nor ass. For they came up with their cattle and their tents, and they came as grasshoppers for multitude; for both they and their camels were without number: and they entered into the land to destroy it. And Israel was greatly impoverished because of the Midianites; and the children of Israel cried unto the LORD."

I cannot find one example in the Bible of a cave experience that was permanent. For each of the cavemen and cave experiences, there was a point of deliverance. There was an exodus. There was a victorious outcome. The caves proved to be beneficial to God's servants through His providential intervention, in time of need.

In Divine providence, each cave proved to be temporary. The caveman of consideration in this sermon, Gideon, grew weary of hiding and ventured out. His family needed provision and deliverance from the tyrannical forces that had driven them to the caves. Gideon might have said and probably would say today, "It is time to get out of the cave!" Don't be discouraged and have the mentality of "I'm just going to stay here for the rest of my life." You should never be confined or isolated as a child of God. To understand the setting of these cave dwellers, let's find the answers to some important questions.

First, consider who were these cave dwellers? In Judges 6:2 we find, "the children of Israel made them the dens which are in the mountains, and caves, and strong holds." These cave dwellers were the descendants of great heritage: a heritage that had given them dwellings in a land flowing with milk and honey. They were descendants of the generation of the children of Israel led by valiant men of faith: Joshua and Caleb, who fought their way into this land. Joshua 24 gives us the stirring message of Joshua when he said, "And if it seem evil unto you to serve the LORD, choose you this day whom ye will serve; whether the gods which your fathers served that were on the other side of the flood, or the gods of the Amorites, in whose land ye dwell: but as for me and my house, we will serve the LORD." Joshua seemed to be warning the generations to follow, that if they forsook the Lord, they could lose this wonderful land.

Hebrews 11 speaks of the great men and women who had paid the price for the liberties of the children of Israel as well as the liberties you and I have in Christ.

"And what shall I more say? For the time would fail me to tell of Gedeon, and of Barak, and of Samson, and of Jephthae; of David also, and Samuel, and of the prophets: Who through faith subdued kingdoms, wrought righteousness, obtained promises, stopped the mouths of lions, Quenched the violence of fire, escaped the edge of the sword, out of weakness were made strong, waxed valiant in fight, turned to flight the armies of the aliens. Women received their dead raised to life again: and others were tortured, not accepting deliverance; that they might obtain a better resurrection: And others had trial of cruel mockings and scourgings, yea, moreover of bonds and imprisonment: They were stoned, they were sawn asunder, were tempted, were slain with the sword: they wandered about in sheepskins and goatskins; being destitute, afflicted, tormented; (Of whom the world was not worthy:) they wandered in deserts, and in mountains, and in dens and caves of the earth. And these all, having obtained a good report through faith, received not the promise" (Hebrews 11:32-39).

Second, why were they dwelling in caves? It was fear. God had given them the land, but now the Midianites, the Amalekites, and the children of the East had come up against them. These fearful foes were of their kindred. They too were descendants of Abraham found in Genesis 25. It seems that some of those within our country are bringing fear to God's people. Our government, media and bureaucrats, have used fear to drive the church into isolation. We are told to report any who refuse to comply fully. We are reminded of Matthew 10:36, "And a man's foes shall be they of his own household."

Paul reminds us in 2 Timothy 1:7, "For God hath not given us the spirit of fear; but of power, and of love, and of a sound mind." Are you afraid? Are you fearful? That's not a spirit of God, for God is not the author of confusion. Satan is the author of confusion and the master of division. He seeks to separate and isolate each of us from other believers in caves of isolation. God is our Commander and our fortification. God commands believers to assemble and encourage each other in the faith (Hebrews 10:24-25).

For many of God's people, God has allowed them to accomplish great things by faith, but perhaps the greatest accomplishment of God's people are those who stayed faithful in spite of great hardships. Hebrews goes on to say that you and I have the rewards for which they gave their lives. That should give us the courage to not compromise, but to take a stand. One day, I will stand before the Lord with those who died for our religious liberties. Our great nation was founded upon the liberty to worship God and follow our faith as we feel God leads us. But, we have yielded our sacred liberties for which those men have died. I have no desire to stand in judgment with those martyrs of freedom, having squandered the liberties that are coming into question today. We will not only face the Lord, but we will stand shoulder to shoulder with those who paid the price for our liberty.

I not only think of those who have sacrificed for our religious liberty, but I think of the national heritage we have received of our forefathers. The signers of the Declaration of Independence knew the risks they were facing. Yet, John Hancock signed his name with large bold strokes so the king would not mistake it. He lost all that he had and the lives of his family for our sacred liberty.

It was at St. John's Church in Richmond, Virginia, on March 23, 1775, that Patrick Henry made his famous speech to the Second Virginia Convention. His speech ended with, "Give me liberty or give me death!"

It was Benjamin Franklin who made the statement, "He who sacrifices liberty for safety deserves neither liberty nor safety."

The founding of this great country was not by those seeking a better welfare or business opportunity, but those seeking a place to serve God!

What caused these descendants of great heritage, who had been given their freedom and blessed promised land, to forsake their liberties fleeing like rats to dens and caves? The dilemma came about by compromise, complacency, and calamity.

God had given them the command of separation and of serving God alone, but they compromised by serving the various gods of the land. (Judges 2:1-3, "And an angel of the LORD came up from Gilgal to Bochim, and said, I made you to go up out of Egypt, and have brought you unto the land which I sware unto your fathers; and I said, I will never break my covenant with you. And ye shall make no league with the inhabitants of this land; ye shall throw down their altars: but ye have not obeyed my voice: why have ye done this? Wherefore I also said, I will not drive them out from before you; but they shall be as thorns in your sides, and their gods shall be a snare unto you.") Verse 10 of that same chapter tells us that after the generations of

Joshua and Caleb, there was a generation who would not continue to serve God.

Soon, calamity followed; they lost it all. "And they encamped against them, and destroyed the increase of the earth, till thou come unto Gaza, and left no sustenance for Israel, neither sheep, nor ox, nor ass" (Judges 6:4).

But then we find the good news: deliverance from the cave. The people in their distress cried out to God. God chose Gideon, a man who had ventured out of the cave, to deliver the children of Israel. I don't know what cave you're in, but God can deliver you out of it.

To get out of the cave, we must seek the face of God.

To get out of the cave, you must first seek God as did the children of Israel. Judges 6:7 says "And it came to pass, when the children of Israel cried unto the LORD because of the Midianites," God sent a prophet to warn them of the error of their ways. In Judges 6:8 we read, "That the LORD sent a prophet unto the children of Israel, which said unto them, Thus saith the LORD God of Israel, I brought you up from Egypt, and brought you forth out of the house of bondage."

God will do the same for us. God has given us men of God to preach repentance to our sinful nation. God has promised, "If my people, which are called by my name, shall humble themselves, and pray, and seek my face, and turn from their wicked ways; then will I hear from heaven, and will forgive their sin, and will heal their land" (2 Chronicles 7:14). God has told us the key to being delivered from our caves is to seek His face.

To get out of the cave, we must surrender to God.

Not only must we seek His face, we must wave the white flag of unconditional surrender. We must yield to Him. Gideon had enough! He determined to get out of the hole he was in. In verses 11-14, we read: "And there came an angel of the LORD, and sat under an oak which was in Ophrah, that pertained unto Joash the Abiezrite: and his son Gideon threshed wheat by the winepress, to hide it from the Midianites. And the angel of the LORD appeared unto him, and said unto him, The LORD is with thee, thou mighty man of valour. And Gideon said unto him, Oh my Lord, if the LORD be with us, why then is all this befallen us? And where be all his miracles which our fathers told us of, saying, Did not the LORD bring us up out of the land of Egypt? But now the LORD hath forsaken us, and delivered us into the hands of the Midianites. And the LORD looked upon him, and said, Go in this thy might, and thou shalt save Israel from the hand of the Midianites: have not I sent thee?"

To get out of the cave, we must be willing to sacrifice.

To get out of our caves, we must not only seek God's face and surrender, but we must also be willing to sacrifice. Notice in verses 18-19, what Gideon did when God had spoken to him: "Depart not hence, I pray thee, until I come unto thee, and bring forth my present, and set it before thee. And he said, I will tarry until thou come again. And Gideon went in, and made ready a kid, and unleavened cakes of an ephah of flour: the flesh he put in a basket, and he put the broth in a pot, and brought it out unto him under the oak, and presented it." Remember, there was very little left in the coffers and the pantry. Yet Gideon made a willing, sacrificial offering. He did not find excuses. What do you have that you'd be willing to give up and give to the Lord? There may be some things that God asks you to sacrifice, but know assuredly, God will bless obedience. Worship the Lord with what you already have, not with what you wish you had!

To get out of the cave, we must be willing to make a separation.

To get out of the cave we must be willing to separate ourselves unto God. Perhaps alone in our caves, God has allowed time for introspection. When you begin to get alone with God, He may show you some things that you need to get rid of that may be interfering with His blessings on your life. God said to Gideon in verses 25-26, "And it came to pass the same night, that the LORD said unto him, Take thy father's young bullock, even the second bullock of seven years old, and throw down the altar of Baal that thy father hath, and cut down the grove that is by it: And build an altar unto the LORD thy God upon the top of this rock, in the ordered place, and take the second bullock, and offer a burnt sacrifice with the wood of the grove which thou shalt cut down." Cut down literally means to cut in pieces. He commanded him to use those idols for kindling and make an altar to give God the preeminence. There shouldn't be anything that comes before God in your life; if there is, it is idolatry. If we are to take back our blessed promised land, we must rid ourselves of anything hiding the face of God. God must have the preeminence.

You need the peace of God about the will of God. God is such a kind, patient, gracious God. Do you realize that He was aware of the doubts and fears that Gideon still had within himself? He wanted Gideon to be assured of

His will and allowed him to put out the fleece (Judges 6:36-40). Make sure you get God's peace about God's will, not just about what you want to do. So often, Christians tell God what they're going to do, then do what they want to do, and call it the will of God. When was the last time you put God to the test and allowed Him to prove Himself to you? God will so often tell you exactly what He wants you to do from the pages of Scripture. I can testify! When you read explicitly from His Word, pray for His will for your petition. The peace of God gives you assurance of His will.

To get out of the cave, we must have solidarity.

To get out of the cave, we must have solidarity (a union or fellowship arising from common responsibility and interest). The devil will try to get you to squabble with others over anything. We find in chapter seven, that Gideon had 32,000 men who God knew would not stick together. God told him he had too many and sent 22,000 of the fearful home. Most of the remaining were careless. God wanted only those who were observant and serious about the task; therefore, He purged the dwindling army until Gideon was left with only three hundred men. God doesn't need many to accomplish His will, but He needs those who will stick together without being fearful or frivolous. God will use the faithful few. If there has ever been a time in our nation and churches that Christians need to come together and seek God, it is now.

To get out of the cave, we must take a stand.

The Bible commands us in Ephesians 6 to "stand against the wiles of the devil" (verse 11) and to "take unto you the whole armour of God, that ye may be able to withstand in the evil day, and having done all, to stand. Stand therefore, having your loins girt about with truth, and having on the breastplate of righteousness" (verses 13-14).

In Judges 7:21 it says, "And they stood every man in his place." God didn't have them carry a sword. They were simply commanded, "Blow the trumpet; break the pitcher; and let the light shine!" God did the rest. Then He said, "Cry aloud." When they obeyed these instructions, God brought about a great victory.

To stay out of the cave, we must be steadfast.

We must be vigilant and stay in the fight. Though we may get weary, we must not quit! (Judges 8:4, "And Gideon came to Jordan, and passed over, he, and the three hundred men that were with him, faint, yet pursuing them.") Gideon and his men pursued and fought all night, and all the next day and night; but before the sun came up the next morning, they had gained the victory! Judges 8:10-13 says, "Now Zebah and Zalmunna were in Karkor, and their hosts with them, about fifteen thousand men, all that were left of all the hosts of the children of the east: for there fell an hundred and twenty thousand men that drew sword. And Gideon went up by the way of them that dwelt in tents on the east of Nobah and Jogbehah, and smote the host: for the host was secure. And when Zebah and Zalmunna fled, he pursued after them, and took the two kings of Midian, Zebah and Zalmunna, and discomfited all the host. And Gideon the son of Joash returned from battle before the sun was up."

So from fear to faith and from little faith to great faith, from wrong to right, from many to few and few to many, from hiding in the dark to standing and shining the light, from being silent to sounding the trumpet, from flight to fight, from a pout to a shout, from faint to mounting up with wings as eagles, from fleeing to pursuing, and from dusk till dawn, from sowing to reaping a harvest, we must just be "steadfast, unmoveable, always abounding in the work of the Lord." God will lead you out of the cave and into victory!

CHAPTER 13
The Cave of Machpelah,

The Cave of Double Portion

"A Mother Laid to Rest"

Genesis 23

"And Sarah was an hundred and seven and twenty years old: these were the years of the life of Sarah. And Sarah died in Kirjatharba; the same is Hebron in the land of Canaan: and Abraham came to mourn for Sarah, and to weep for her. And Abraham stood up from before his dead, and spake unto the sons of Heth, saying I am a stranger and a sojourner with you: give me a possession of a buryingplace with you, that I may bury my dead out of my sight. And the children of Heth answered Abraham, saying unto him, Hear us, my lord: thou art a mighty prince among us: in the choice of our sepulchres bury thy dead; none of us shall withhold from thee his sepulchre, but that thou mayest bury thy dead. And Abraham stood up, and bowed himself to the people of the land, even to the children of Heth. And he communed with them, saying, If it be your mind that I should bury my dead out of my sight; hear me, and intreat for me to Ephron the son of Zohar, That he may give me the cave of Machpelah, which he hath, which is in the end of his field; for as much money as it is worth he shall give it me for a possession of a buryingplace amongst you. And Ephron dwelt among the children of Heth: and Ephron the Hittite answered

Abraham in the audience of the children of Heth, even of all that went in at the gate of his city, saying, Nay, my lord, hear me: the field give I thee, and the cave that is therein, I give it thee; in the presence of the sons of my people give I it thee: bury thy dead. And Abraham bowed down himself before the people of the land. And he spake unto Ephron in the audience of the people of the land, saying, But if thou wilt give it, I pray thee, hear me: I will give thee money for the field; take it of me, and I will bury my dead there. And Ephron answered Abraham, saying unto him, My lord, hearken unto me: the land is worth four hundred shekels of silver; what is that betwixt me and thee? bury therefore thy dead. And Abraham hearkened unto Ephron; and Abraham weighed to Ephron the silver, which he had named in the audience of the sons of Heth, four hundred shekels of silver, current money with the merchant. And the field of Ephron, which was in Machpelah, which was before Mamre, the field, and the cave which was therein, and all the trees that were in the field, that were in all the borders round about, were made sure Unto Abraham for a possession in the presence of the children of Heth, before all that went in at the gate of his city. And after this, Abraham buried Sarah his wife in the cave of the field of Machpelah before Mamre: the same is Hebron in the land of Canaan. And the field, and the cave that is therein, were made sure unto Abraham for a possession of a buryingplace by the sons of Heth."

There are times in life when we are in desperate need of God's grace. God has promised for His children, grace for every need, for every trial. This cave experience is of the passing of a dear mother and the story of her being laid to rest.

Visit the Scene

I would first like to describe to you the scene of this cave experience. The place is Hebron, which had been known (as we find in verse 2) as Kirjatharba, "The City of the Four Giants." These giants were the sons of Arba. When I think about who this giant was in type, I think of the devil. And if I named his four sons in type, I would name them: The Giant of Sin, The Giant of Death, The Giant of Corruption, and the Giant of Hell. This was known as the possession of the giant.

But it became known as Hebron, which means "the seat of association." It became known as an association or a society of people. Today, our courthouse is a place where our society has legality: the place where we settle our affairs. It is a place of records, such as marriage licenses and death certificates. At this place, a transaction was made that changed its name, previously known for its fearful adversaries, to being known as the place of a new, peaceful society. Today, we celebrate a transaction that took place at Calvary!

Sympathize their Sorrows

It was there, inside a tent, that an ancient man bent over a frail, lifeless body of a truly lovely princess. He is sobbing. Heartbroken. His tears falling upon the still lovely face of the one he had loved for over a century. These tears would not awaken this "Sleeping Beauty"! But this is no Disney fairy tale. This princess had been blessed with the beauty of Heaven, and God Himself had given her the name, "Princess." The ancient man is Father Abraham, and this princess is his wife, Sarah. I read a document from an ancient, Jewish historian, Josephus, who said that, even at her death, she still had her stunning beauty. When God touched Abraham and Sarah, He restored their youth unto them.

Standing nearby is the momma's boy of 37 years with tears streaming down his face. He had not experienced life without his dear mother! This dear mother had been the only love of his life. The sorrow was overwhelming. These men, and all of their clan, were pilgrims and strangers in a strange land. They had wandered looking for a great city "whose builder and maker is God" (Hebrews 11:8-10). For the moment, the journey seemed to have ended for them here in Hebron.

The Grim Reaper of Death had traced the steps of Father Time, the steps which ended, not in a marble palace, but in a simple tent of a shepherdess. Death had summoned "Corruption" to drag his lifeless victim away into oblivion.

Oh! The sorrow of Death, this unwelcome intruder that had come! Yet, this unwelcome guest had been invited by a villain. The villain was Sin (Genesis 2:17; Romans 6:23). Death had caused separation. Adam and Eve experienced separation from all they held dear and sacred as they were driven from the Garden of Eden.

Abraham knew that Sarah would never be able to speak with him again in this life, prepare a meal for him, or tell him she loved him again. It would never be the same again. The same is true for each of us, because the "wages of sin is death" (Romans 6:23). The best synonym for death is separation. It's not ceasing to exist or annihilation, but separation. Paul said in 2 Corinthians 5:8, "to be absent from the body, and to be present with the Lord." For those who do not know Jesus as their Savior, it is a hopeless separation. This sorrow is the "sting of death" (1 Corinthians 15:56). It is as piercing as the sting of a serpent's bite.

Abraham stood up from his sorrow.

When sorrow comes, there must be a time when we choose to stand up. God's precious promises must be stood upon. I can hear Abraham exclaim, "For this corruptible must put on incorruption, and this mortal must put on immortality. So when this corruptible shall have put on incorruption, and this mortal shall have put on immortality, then shall be brought to pass the saying that is written, Death is swallowed up in victory. O death, where is thy sting? O grave, where is thy victory?" (I Corinthians 15:53-55).

"And Abraham stood up from before his dead..." (Genesis 23:3). Death is not final for those who have the promise of God. Death stood saying, "I'm ready to take her. This is final." But then God said to Abraham, "I am here. I will never leave you, nor forsake you. My Word is true! My promise is true!" God has promised this same grace for every need and every sorrow. That grace overwhelmed Abraham, and he stood up with a change of behavior and emotion. He stood up, by faith, upon the promises of God. The wonderful truth for those who have died in the Lord is that we can sing, "I'll see you again, I'll see you again...I'll see you in glory someday!" ("Precious in the sight of the LORD is the death of his saints." Psalm 116:15)

The Sepulcher He Sought

Like most people, Abraham hadn't made preparations for this time of separation. He stood up from his sorrow! It seems God spoke to him, "I would not have you to be ignorant, brethren, concerning them which are asleep, that ye sorrow not, even as others which have no hope." A burying place had to be sought, a significant place. A place where the generations to follow could have a burying place of significance and identity. A great transaction had to be made with the children of Arba, "The Giant." Abraham bought a place: the Cave of Machpelah, "The Cave of a Double Portion." His sorrow and his Sarah must be laid to rest.

Likewise, for there to be a future for each of us, a great transaction had to be made with the children of "The Giant." Jesus sought and bought, with His precious blood, the place of double portion. The promise of a double portion was not recorded in Hebron, "The Place of Society," but in Heaven, "The Place of the Redeemed Society!" Jesus purchased a place of redemption, but also a promise of resurrection!

This cave would be where the society of Abraham would be settled. It would become a testimony of God's promise. The first to be laid here would be Sarah.

Yes! He sought and he bought, but he also wrought a heritage, a mark, a place distinctively known as his. Time and time again throughout the Bible, we read "Abraham, Isaac, and Jacob." Jacob gathered his family together to give them his last words, and in Genesis 49:29-33 said, "I am to be gathered unto my people: bury me with my fathers in the cave that is in the field of Ephron the Hittite, In the cave that is in the field of Machpelah, which is before Mamre, in the land of Canaan, which Abraham bought with the field of Ephron the Hittite for a possession of a buryingplace. There they buried Abraham and Sarah his wife; there they buried Isaac and Rebecca his wife; and there I buried Leah. The purchase of the field and of the cave that is therein was from the children of Heth. And when Jacob had made an end of commanding his sons, he gathered up his feet into the bed, and yielded up the ghost, and was gathered unto his people." It was a testimony that Abraham had left behind. In the New Testament, Jesus referenced Abraham and the heritage of two places: one goodly and one evil. The heritage of a lost man and the heritage of a saved man. "And it came to pass, that the beggar died, and was carried by the angels into Abraham's bosom: the rich man also died, and was buried; And in hell he lift up his eyes, being in torments, and seeth Abraham afar off, and Lazarus in his bosom" (Luke 16:22-23). Just as Abraham, each of us will have a testimony that will be left behind.

This place of double portion signified rest. Revelation 14:13 says, "And I heard a voice from heaven saying unto me, Write, Blessed are the dead which die in the Lord from henceforth: Yea, saith the Spirit, that they may rest from their labours; and their works do follow them." We can know that when our loved ones go on beyond our eyesight, we may not be able to see them, but they are at rest, just as Sarah was.

The double portion is a place of rest, but it is also a place of resurrection (2 Corinthians 5:8). Jesus told Mary and Martha in John 11:25-26, "I am the resurrection, and the life: he that believeth in me, though he were dead, yet shall he live: And whosoever liveth and believeth in me shall never die." You may be weeping. You may be stooping and bending down in the cave that you're in, but you can stand up, because there's a better day coming!